T0117663

THE
PRACTICAL
GUIDE
TO # EXCEPTIONAL
LIVING

Creating AND *Living* THE *Life* OF *Your Dreams*

JIM GARLAND

New York

The Practical Guide To Exceptional Living
Creating and Living the Life of Your Dreams

Copyright © 2010 Jim Garland. All rights reserved.

No part of this publication may be reproduced or transmitted in any form or by any means, mechanical or electronic, including photocopying and recording, or by any information storage and retrieval system, without permission in writing from the author or publisher (except by a reviewer, who may quote brief passages and/or short brief video clips in a review.)

Disclaimer: The Publisher and the Author make no representations or warranties with respect to the accuracy or completeness of the contents of this work and specifically disclaim all warranties, including without limitation warranties of fitness for a particular purpose. No warranty may be created or extended by sales or promotional materials. The advice and strategies contained herein may not be suitable for every situation. This work is sold with the understanding that the Publisher is not engaged in rendering legal, accounting, or other professional services. If professional assistance is required, the services of a competent professional person should be sought. Neither the Publisher nor the Author shall be liable for damages arising herefrom. The fact that an organization or website is referred to in this work as a citation and/or a potential source of further information does not mean that the Author or the Publisher endorses the information the organization or website may provide or recommendations it may make. Further, readers should be aware that internet websites listed in this work may have changed or disappeared between when this work was written and when it is read.

Cover Design by: Rachel Lopez
                           Rachel@r2cdesign

ISBN 978-1-60037-716-7

Library of Congress Control Number: 2009936846

MORGAN · JAMES
THE ENTREPRENEURIAL PUBLISHER

Morgan James Publishing, LLC
1225 Franklin Ave., STE 325
Garden City, NY 11530-1693
Toll Free 800-485-4943
www.MorganJamesPublishing.com

In an effort to support local communities, raise awareness and funds, Morgan James Publishing donates one percent of all book sales for the life of each book to Habitat for Humanity. Get involved today, visit **www.HelpHabitatForHumanity.org.**

Dedication

I dedicate this book to my wife Carrie and our four wonderful children Bayley, Ellie, Jack, and Benjamin.

Carrie has been the love of my life since high school. She is the woman who has made me the man I am today, my soul mate and truly my best friend. She is the person who brings me my greatest happiness and joy. Carrie's love and support are the only reason that this book became a reality. Her experience in journalism helped as well, as she was my first (and toughest) editor! She is the best mother a child and husband could ever imagine - she is patient, fun, energetic, kind, and adventurous. I love you.

Bayley, you have been such a delight since the day you were born that we decided to have three more kids! Your great attitude, sense of humor and smarts are inspirational. I love you and cherish all of the joy you have brought to mommy and me.

Ellie, watching you grow up has brought more joy to my life than you will ever know. You are spunky, funny, and smart as a whip and I adore you for that. I love you and will forever hold onto the excitement you have given mommy and me.

Jack, it is a blessing to have you as my son. Your varied interests amaze me and your sense of humor makes me laugh until I can't breathe. I love you and cherish the conversations, the fun and the laughter you bring to mommy and me.

Benjamin, you are a delight to behold, with a twinkle in your eye and a spring in your step. Jimmy Buffet and Bob Marley would be proud to hear you sing along to any of their songs. I love you to the moon and back and thank you for the happiness you bring mommy and me.

I also dedicate this book to my late mom (Dickey), my late Pop (Jake), my late sister (Karen), my brother Joe and my sisters Leslie and Felicia. I have shared more joy, laughter and adventure with all of you than the law should allow. Your support of my crazy ideas has given me the strength I have found when the odds have been against me. You have all brought love, passion and excitement to my life. The adventures we shared as children - camping, fishing, going to the beach, Uncle Tommy's, traveling in an RV, and simply playing together - are etched in my memory forever. The pleasure of sharing these things with you makes me the luckiest guy in the world. With all of my love, I thank you.

Acknowledgements

I wish to acknowledge and thank the following people for giving me the strength, resources and passion for shaping my life and bringing this book to reality:

- **Carrie, Bayley, Ellie, Jack and Benjamin,** *for the unbelievable patience, help, ideas and strength you have provided for me on this journey.*

- **PJ Maher, Sharp Details, Inc. Operations Manager,** *for teaching me to simplify, to look at the big picture, to be patient and think things through before making a snap judgment or decision. You have allowed me to work on my strengths and grow the business while you use your strengths to handle the day-to-day details and refine our operating systems. You have a management team that would make Warren Buffet proud. You have given me the freedom to develop relationships with our clients and thereby exceed our business goals.*

- **Christina Miller, Sharp Details, Inc. Office Operations Guru,** *for organizing and simplifying what was chaos and for keeping my "shoot from the hip style" in check. If I need something you have it, if*

I have lost something you find it and if it is technical you guide me through it. You manage to keep our accounts receivable on time and up-to-date which is the life blood of our business. You are the best!

– **Tom Dula, Sharp Details, Inc. CFO,** *for your passion and care for our business, your ability to turn the financially complex into something I understand and your friendship. Thank you for steering us in the right direction and for helping me turn Sharp Details into a financially sound and profitable business.*

– **Ed Behling, Cindy Bailey, Janet Carbajal, Brian Dower, Colleen Mascara, Eric Pulling, Mike Vinaya, Will Zimdars, Sharp Details, Inc. Management Team**, *your leadership ability, professionalism, customer service, attention to detail, hard work, countless hours, patience, creativity and dedication continue to exceed what I ever thought imaginable. It is what you do, day in and day out that has allowed our company to grow and serve so many in our wonderful industry. It is an honor and a privilege to share this with you. Not a day goes by that I don't thank the Lord for bringing you to Sharp Details, Inc. Your loyalty and friendship mean the world to me.*

– **The Sharp Details, Inc. Service Technicians,** *thanks to the men and women who keep our customers happy, our managers sane and the nuts and bolts of the business running all day, every day. Your dedication,* *hard work and loyalty are not always praised but are always appreciated. Thank you, Gracias!*

‒ **Ann McIndoo,** *for your, ideas, guidance, resources, and business process. Your ability to take my mixed-up, disorganized, and rambling ideas and concepts and help me turn them into a book has been amazing.*

‒ **David Farber, of Patton and Boggs, LLP,** *for your tenacity, professionalism, wit and for guiding me through one of the toughest periods of my business career.*

‒ **Sharp Details, Inc.'s clients and friends,** *for your dedication, continued business and friendship. A special thanks to Gene Condreras of Panorama Flight Service for encouraging me to branch out from my core business. You are the greatest clients in the world. I have made more lifelong friends in this industry than I ever could have imagined. The work we all do is challenging, demanding and sometimes unforgiving and we love it! My heartfelt thanks to all of you. Special thanks to Joe Tate, who gave me the opportunity to get into this great industry and to Bill Maynard, who first taught me to clean an aircraft!*

‒ **Carroll and Patty Owens**, *for never doubting me when I wanted to marry your daughter and promised to take good care of her, and for always making me feel part of the family. Your support is a blessing.*

– *My Friends* *from Bush Hill Elementary, Thomas Edison High School, Radford University, New River Valley and Radford Rugby clubs, to Phi Sigma Kappa, the Chart House, Barnacle Jim's Boat Service, Sharp Details, Inc., Rehoboth, St Aidan's, St John's, Riverside Gardens, Grace Episcopal (Jim, Brian, Tony, Phil, Bob, Ken and all of your lovely brides), Belle Haven, Surfing (Ross and Dave) and beyond. I thank you all for making me laugh so hard that my stomach is sore the next day, giving me memories that will be with me forever, providing me with inspiration and guidance, causing me to raise my standards, improve my surfing and my golf game and most of all for just being good friends that I can count on for the rest of my life. You guys and gals are the greatest friends I could ever ask for!*

Contents

Introduction

I always thought I was someone who tried to strive for excellence in my life. The problem was I never really had the discipline to make the changes that would bring about that excellence. In high school, I played football and did okay, but during the off-season I was not dedicated to staying in shape. Instead of striving for excellence, I would just hang out with my buddies. We had fun, but none of us thought about doing what it would take to play sports beyond high school.

The same was true with my study habits. I could do well, but instead of striving for excellence I cruised through with a low B average and never really thought much about it. As I moved on to college, things did not change. I attended Radford University in Radford, Virginia from the fall of 1986 until my graduation in the spring of 1990. I had fun, made terrific lifelong friends, played rugby, and coasted through with a C average. I will never forget the frustration of my math economics professor, Dr. Kasturi. I was an economics major and needed a C in his class in order to graduate. We had two tests: the midterm and the final. I bombed the midterm with a 34 (yes, out of 100). Before the final, several of us got together and studied around the clock. After the final, I went to Dr. Kasturi's office to see if I was going to be able to graduate. In his classic Indian accent he said, "Mr. Garland, I do not understand people like you. You have the ability to do so well, but it is like you do not care. You got a 105 on the final—the highest grade in the class. Your average is a 69.9 and I will give you a C." I was thrilled. He was not.

He basically posed the question, "Why are you such an underachiever?" At that moment, I realized I had not been striving for excellence but settling for mediocrity. I realized that although I had fleeting thoughts of success I had always accepted mediocrity as the norm. That was a turning point in my life.

Like many of you, I wanted a life of joy, success, loving relationships, financial stability, adventure and excitement. Since then I have had several defining moments in my life, turning points, that caused me to look at where I was and make the decision to turn it up a notch.

What will be the defining moment in your life? When will you no longer settle for mediocrity? When are you going to decide to start designing the life of your dreams? Is now the time?

Since that time with Dr. Kasturi, more than 20 years ago, I have focused much of my energy on studying what actions people take who truly create the lives that they want—people who truly strive for excellence. Throughout this process, I have read hundreds of books, listened to countless hours of tapes and CDs, watched videos, attended seminars, enrolled in classes for entrepreneurs, hired personal trainers and coaches and visited, analyzed and learned from countless websites. As a result, I have purposely designed my life and my business to be exactly what I want it to be.

Here are a few examples:

– I married Carrie, my high school sweetheart and the woman of my dreams.

- *We have been blessed with four beautiful children: Bayley, Ellie, Jack and Benjamin.*
- *Our children attend schools that we love.*
- *We live in a wonderful house in a beautiful neighborhood.*
- *I have grown my business, Sharp Details, Inc., from the trunk of my car (as a boat cleaning service) into a company that produces almost $4,000,000 in annual revenue, providing aircraft detailing, cleaning and support services, operates in eight different states with over 50 employees, and runs without my day-to-day involvement.*
- *I work out regularly, enjoy great health, and can still fit into the tuxedo I bought for my wedding 14 years ago!*
- *I take 10 weeks of vacation per year (no contact at all with the office) and spend much of my time with my wife and kids.*

*My aim in writing **The Practical Guide to Exceptional Living** is to give you a simple book, a guide that can help you along the way. It is packed with ideas that will save you years of trial-and-error and gives you the tools and philosophy you need to begin your journey towards creating and living the life of your dreams. You can make the changes in your life you have always wanted to make, **today**… and I will show you how!*

Warm regards,

Jim Garland

Chapter One
Are You Living the Life of Your Dreams?

*"Go confidently in the direction of your
dreams, live the life you have imagined."*
Henry David Thoreau (1817-1862)
American author, poet, and philosopher

Are you living the life of your dreams? What would the life of your dreams look like? How would you envision it? Many people shy away from these questions because they are so direct; they really hit you in the gut and make you start to think and that is the idea. I want to get you thinking about what the answers to these very direct questions should be and how you would describe, in detail, the life of your dreams. You must know what you want and where you want to go. Answering these questions is where the journey begins.

By the end of this book you will have developed a new strategy for how you look at life and a game plan for deliberately designing the life you desire on every level. The subjects on the following pages will help you define what it means to have a truly exceptional life. As you read, think about how these subjects relate to your daily life.

Time: Your Most Valuable Asset

At the beginning of my business career, I was taught by my colleagues that working long, hard hours was not only necessary but was required as a means to success. It was almost like a badge of honor to work 80-90 hours per week. If you wanted to succeed you had to put in the hours at any cost and if you didn't, you were not worthy. As I began my journey as a small business owner, I focused on two things:

1. Work as many hours as humanly possible
2. Accumulate as much money as humanly possible

As shallow as it seems, that was it. Work hard to make money. I was 21 and single and this seemed like a great philosophy. What it actually produced was a very tired body and mind, a business that could not be left for five minutes without my hands in everything, a girlfriend, and family and friends who wanted to know why I worked so much. Unfortunately for me, I had put no value on time and measured my success by how many hours I worked. This is a sure formula for failure on every level and I was proving it to myself.

As time went on and my business continued to grow, I realized more and more that the additional hours I was working were becoming less and less productive. It was at this point that I realized I had to let go of some of the responsibilities of the business and allow others to take charge. To delegate effectively you need patience, trial and error with many different people and a willingness to understand that many mistakes will be made and corrected, along the way. It was one of the hardest things I have ever had to do; however, as months and years passed, I became more effective at building business systems and designing clear divisions of authority and responsibility. My business continued to grow, I began to gain more and more control over my time and more of my employees improved their management and leadership skills.

Thanks to delegating successfully, my philosophy and life have changed 180 degrees. I now believe that time is the most valuable commodity I have and how I spend it is paramount. I no longer work weekends or 80 hours a week. Don't get me wrong, I could. I just have chosen not to, and with that choice have designed my business and my life so I control how I spend my time. How did I do it? How is this possible? I made a deliberate decision to redesign my life and business. I have assembled an unbelievable team at my company, Sharp Details, Inc. and it is this team that has been built over many years, that has allowed me the benefit of spending my time as I choose.

The amazing thing is that since I have set the business up in this way and delegated tasks I am not good at (in an effort to achieve personal freedom) my business has improved tremendously. It runs more efficiently without my hands in everything, it provides jobs for more people, it serves our customers better, and it generates greater revenue than ever. I have finally begun to achieve true success. To me, that means having the ability to spend my time the way I want to spend it. This control over my time has allowed me the flexibility to spend valuable time with my wife Carrie, our children and at the same time, grow my company 30% per year over the last three years. It has provided me with the luxury of being able to pursue other interests including creating a foundation, starting a new company and writing this book. I also have plenty of opportunity for recreational activities I enjoy, such as traveling with my family and surfing and golfing with my buddies.

The average person will spend 110,000 hours of their life on their career (commuting and working 50 hours per week for a 44 year career from the age of 21-65). This means you spend more time working and commuting than you will ever spend with your family. Is this what you want? Do you so love your job or your business that you would spend this much time at it, or do you need to make a change? Outside of work, the time you spend with others is another critical amount of time you should analyze. Who are you spending your time with? Do you hang out with people who support you and give you encouragement on a daily basis? Are they positive and fun?

What about your loved ones? Most of us spend time planning for work, exercise, special events, dinner and a host of other things. How much time do you actively plan to spend with your loved ones or do they just get whatever time is leftover?

To design the life of your dreams, you must gain control of your time. This is the first step and here are six guidelines to help you get started. They will help you begin thinking about how you spend your time. Remember, your time is your most valuable asset and it is the biggest factor in designing the life of your dreams.

1. Start every day with a plan. I write my daily plan on an index card every night before I go to bed. This keeps you organized and on task.

2. Ask your workplace to offer you opportunities to work from home, or pay you for your results instead of your time.

3. Ask your workplace to offer you flexible hours. Maybe you can go in early some days and late on others.

4. Explore opportunities/companies that offer jobs working from home utilizing today's technology.

5. Manage how you communicate:
   - Turn off all email alerts on your computer and phone.
   - Put your phone on vibrate.
   - Put an auto response on your email letting others know you will respond at certain times or days so they do not expect an immediate response.
   - Plan time with your spouse and kids first, and then fill in around that.
   - Designate 1-2 days per week that you do not check email or work phone.
   - At dinners out, ball games, and special events leave your communication device in the car.

6. Before making commitments to others, ask these questions: Do I like being with this person? Do they make me feel good? Do we have fun together? If you answer "no" to any of these questions, rethink spending time with this person. If you

answer "no" and you are married to this person, get professional help! Life is too short to spend time feeling angst towards the person you have married.

How is Your Health?

Good health is essential for achieving and living a life that is full of joy and happiness. Good health will provide you with the stamina to face life's challenges, the energy to play, and the stamina to take a long walk. It will give you a mental awareness and strength that can only be discovered when you are in good shape. It will also give you the energy to balance your time between family, work, social commitments, and travel. Most of all, great health will provide you with longevity and extra years that will allow you to more fully enjoy all of life's pleasures.

For any of you who have been overweight and then been disciplined enough to lose it and get in shape, you know there is no comparison between how you feel at your ideal weight and how you felt when you are heavy. *Imagine yourself enjoying working out five days per week, eating fruits and vegetables (colorful and vibrant), getting plenty of rest, reducing your stress and being your ideal body weight. Ladies, imagine getting into your size 6-8 jeans you haven't worn since high school!* Just the description of this makes you feel good. *Now imagine yourself 30 pounds overweight, always tired, eating a regular diet of french fries, burgers and cookies (brown, bland, mushy, greasy), getting no exercise, wearing clothes that don't fit and always exhausted from lack of sleep.* Now, how do you feel? You see your health and weight immediately affect you mentally as well as physically. Most people don't get this.

The biggest reason I work out five to six days per week, eat a diet of fresh fruits and vegetables, limit any kind of prescription drugs, drink plenty of water, try to sleep at least six-plus hours every night, quit chewing tobacco after 25 years, and try to stay as close to my ideal weight as possible is simple. Why? **I want to live as long as possible**. Have you ever thought about this? How long do you want to live? One of my sisters was killed at 19 in an alcohol-related automobile accident. My mom was a heavy smoker and died at age 53 from cancer. It is heartbreaking to think of all of the things they missed because of poor *choices* in lifestyle: so many birthdays, ball games, dance recitals, grandchildren, weddings, baptisms, family gatherings, sunsets, and adventure. I want you to think long and hard about your current lifestyle.

Will you be here to see your children mature and grow old? Will you be here to watch them raise their families and pursue their dreams? Will you be here to enjoy and support them? Be honest with yourself. Are you going to make it to see the grandkids? Or are you going to be gone from this earth because of poor health brought on by poor choices. How is your health?

Achieving the life of your dreams will require energy. You should want as many extra years as possible to enjoy. You are also going to need the self confidence that comes with looking and feeling your best.

Here are a few statistics to think about:

- – The average American female lives to be 77 years old, the average male 73.

- Smoking cigarettes can take an average of 10 years off of your life.
- Being overweight by 20-30 pounds can take an extra five years off of your life.
- According to the CDC (Centers for Disease Control), heart disease is the number - one killer in America. One person dies every minute from a heart attack.
- Being overweight by 20-30 pounds can increase your risk of heart disease, cancer, diabetes, and other weight related diseases. Obesity (being more than 20% over your ideal body weight) greatly increases the risk.
- The average male exercises 1.5 times per week and the average female 1.1 times per week. Sixty minutes of exercise five days per week is recommended.

How Are Your Relationships?

Those who have achieved great things in life most likely have not done so by themselves. They have had the help of many different relationships, usually involving a spouse, business partners, work colleagues and friends. You need support from a variety of people, and that requires you to maintain healthy relationships. How are your relationships? Are they caring and loving and supportive? Do they give you inspiration and energy or do they drain you of your energy? Are they filled with anxiety and stress? Are they antagonistic?

If you are married or have a significant other in your life, this is the most important relationship to help you achieve the things you want in life. You must constantly work at this relationship through the inevitable disagreements, arguments, good times and bad times. It will get stronger as you go. What I find with many people is that they don't understand how much you need to work on a relationship. The couples I have seen that are the happiest are constantly communicating with each other, not always agreeing, but constantly communicating. This is critical, especially in a day and age when there are so many distractions.

Relationships take time, commitment and most of all patience. What was the last thing you said to your spouse before you left today? When was the last time you showed up with flowers or a gift for no reason? When was the last time you told your spouse how beautiful or handsome they were? We often forget these simple gestures because "life" tends to get in the way. Work, email, the kids' schedules and many other commitments occupy our time. As I said earlier, one of the first steps is that you must look at how you truly spend your time. After you do this, you must first schedule time for yourself, your family and your spouse. Then think about friends, old and new. Call them, email them, or invite them for dinner. Go out of your way to be loving and kind to the people you care about most.

My wife often reminds our children, "We are here on earth for one reason and that is to help others and make others feel good." I remember the first time she said this, and I realized that I had never looked at it like that. If everyone went out each day with this philosophy, can you imagine how your relationships with all those around you (including complete strangers) would change? The purpose of our relationships is to help others reach their highest potential and to nurture one another to reach our goals.

We also need others to be around us to give us a sense of worth and a reason to rise each day. We need that sense of camaraderie as humans. Remember this as you leave in the morning to go to work and you look into the eyes of your spouse or children or you wave to your neighbor. We need a connection to other human beings. When you think of the people you have relationships with, think about what you can do for them, not what they need to do for you. And by doing this, you will find that they will help you along the way to create the life you want.

How Is Your Faith?

My faith is a big part of who I am and is an important part of my relationship with my family, especially my children. Your belief is what it is. If your belief is strong, I encourage you to nurture it. If you have no belief or very little, I encourage you to try to discover it. My faith in God and the strength that faith gives me has allowed me to overcome seemingly insurmountable obstacles and taken me from a place of fear and failure to a place of absolute joy and success.

My faith in God gives me the strength to be a loving father and husband, business owner, friend, and good citizen of this great country. My belief has helped me through the deaths of a sister and both of my parents. It has provided me strength when my business was on the verge of going bankrupt and was under siege from a lawsuit. And most of all, God and my belief in God bring me great joy on a beautiful spring day when all is going perfectly. When I look at my beautiful family and all of the joy that nature and my many friends bring, who else can receive the credit but God?

I want you to give great thought to your faith and what it means to you and those around you. We will discuss gratitude and faith to a greater degree in Chapter Three. For now, answer the question, how is your faith?

What Is Important to YOU?

To design the life you have always wanted or to make any positive change in your life you have to know what is important to you. Many people will say that their family is important to them, but then they will work 80 hours per week and not spend time with their family. Or someone will say their health is important, but then they will not do anything to support good health. So, what is important to you? Is it the accumulation of toys and possessions or is it the accumulation of experiences that you share with those around you? I used to struggle with this until a good friend of mine posed a question to me one day. I now call it the Christmas Gift Question.

As I talked with my friend David Allen, describing the book I was writing, we discussed a struggle I was having. I explained to him that I had a lot of ambitious business goals and like to own nice things and have the ability to travel, but that was causing a strain on my family and my relationships. The conflict I faced was the choice between spending time with my family and pursuing my business goals. With that, he hit me with the following question: it is what I call **The Christmas Gift Question**.

"Tell me one gift you remember getting for Christmas each year as a kid from the age of five to fifteen," David said. I stammered for a moment, not being able to think of any, and then I did manage to remember getting skis one Christmas when I was probably about seven and the football game with the guys that would vibrate up and down the field and the field goal kicker that you hit on the head. That was all that I could clearly remember over ten years of Christmas during my childhood.

Then he said, "Describe the vacations and experiences you and your family shared each year from the age of five to fifteen. What were some of the adventures you had?" Instantly my memory was triggered and a whole host of things came back to me. I started to describe all of the great experiences I had as a child growing up in Alexandria, VA: The summer trip my family made in a Winnebago down the east coast, the trips to our condo at Fenwick Island, DE, camping trips to Cave Mountain Lake, VA and the Great Smokey Mountains, trips to visit relatives in Roanoke, VA, the Riverside Hotel in Gatlinburg, TN and staying in the tree houses at Disney World. It was all so vivid and clear. I told him about my dad coaching baseball and my mom being the den mother of my Cub Scout troop. I could have talked for hours about all of the experiences I had growing up.

Thanks to David it then became crystal clear. **Life is about the experiences we have along the way not about the accumulation of things.** Life is about the experiences we share with our families and other loved ones.

This in a broad sense has become my mantra: *Live as long as possible in order to share experiences with the people you love being around!* When you think about this, it is so simple. Isn't this what you want? (If it isn't, close this book and go get your money back!) Think about what has been important to you in your life. Has it been about the accumulation of things or has it been about the experience? Which is more important to you? What changes do you need to make?

The purpose of this chapter has been to get you thinking about your life and what it has become up to this point. As we get older and our commitments expand, our creativity decreases and our dreams somehow begin to fade into the background. The next two exercises are designed to get you thinking BIG again. These exercises are the first steps, the building blocks, in the journey to design or redesign the life of your dreams.

Ultimate Life Experience™

What is your **Ultimate Life Experience**™? What is the one thing you have always wanted to do or the one place you have always wanted to visit? It may be a trip around the world, surfing in Indonesia, going to London to watch Wimbledon, traveling to Korea to visit relatives, going to the World Series, or maybe organizing a family reunion that brings together hundreds of family members. Right now, I challenge you to consider your **Ultimate Life Experience**™, write it down and include steps needed to achieve it. Whatever it is, I want you to think BIG! Dream and plan as if money were not an obstacle. Don't put limits on what you want to do, just think about it as if there was nothing holding you back.

Thinking BIG is the key and here is why. When you begin to think BIG and dream BIG you force yourself to step out of your comfort zone. For example, driving to the beach for the weekend or going to Fiji for two weeks are two completely different goals that you will think about and plan for differently. The weekend trip may be fun, but the trip to Fiji would conjure up a whole different type of excitement and drive. Your mind will become engaged and creative when the goal is BIG. You will have to think about the financial commitment, logistical aspects, and the time constraints that go along with a big goal. You will be forced to break it down into smaller, manageable chunks over time in order to achieve your **Ultimate Life Experience**™. Most importantly, when the goal and dream are bigger than anything you have ever accomplished, so is the excitement level, and it is this excitement level and the feelings you will have when the goal is accomplished that will push you to go for it!

The Legacy Goal™

In this chapter, I have talked about the importance of how you spend your time, your health, your relationships, your faith, your experiences, and what is truly important to you. Hopefully you have begun to think about your first big goal, your **Ultimate Life Experience**™. Your next assignment is creating your **Legacy Goal**™.

How do you want to be remembered? What do you want your legacy to be? While I was going through a program called The *E-Myth* by Michael Gerber www.e-myth.com (an excellent read for entrepreneurs), I was asked to write my own eulogy. This is an interesting exercise and you can start by answering these questions: How will people remember you? How would you want to be remembered? What were some of your accomplishments? What are some of the things you have not accomplished yet, but would like to so they could be part of your eulogy? What one sentence or phrase could sum up the person you have been? The person you would like to be? When you have attended funerals, what was said about the deceased that stuck with you? One piece of advice before you start this: think about what you can do in the next 20-40-60 years that could make your eulogy truly amazing. Think about how you could alter someone's life for the better or the impact you could have on your children. What lessons could you teach or learn over the rest of your life that could be life changing for you and those around you? There is no better time than the present to begin thinking about the rest of your life and the legacy you want to leave behind.

When I think about my **Legacy Goal™**, I immediately think of two things: my children and charitable organizations. First and foremost, the responsibility I have to the world is to leave it with four generous, loving and thoughtful individuals that are always thinking of ways to help others. Four people who have always done their best to have a positive impact on the world, value education, and are constantly looking for ways to show respect and gratitude towards mankind. As a parent, I feel that the biggest contribution I can make to society is to make sure that my children have been raised in a way to value their faith, God, education and respect for themselves and others.

My second biggest responsibility is to provide for others in need, especially those who are trying to better their lives, health, education, or just want a chance to prove themselves, but do not have the means or support to fulfill their dreams. As you begin to develop your **Legacy Goal™,** it is important to think of others and not yourself.

Chapter One Summary
Are You Living the Life of Your Dreams?

Key Points to Remember

- Discovering what The Life of Your Dreams would mean in detail is the cornerstone for making positive change in your life.

- You must know what you want and where you want to go before the journey can begin.

- Time is your most important and valuable asset and how you spend it is critical.

- Vibrant health gives you the energy to pursue your dreams.

- Healthy relationships are critical to your well-being.

- Your spiritual faith and belief are critical in assisting you with creating the life of your dreams!

- Discovering what is truly important to you will guide you to make the right decisions in life.

- Life is about the experiences we share with others, not about the accumulation of material things—The Christmas Gift Question.

- <u>The Ultimate Life Experience</u>™ - Describe in detail what this would be for you and how it would feel to experience this. It could be a trip, vacation, event, or health goal. Forget all obstacles and dream BIG!

- <u>The Legacy Goal</u>™ - How do you want to be remembered? What do you want your legacy to be? What positive impact could you leave on your children, your family, and the world?

Go to
<u>www.thepracticalguidetoexceptionalliving.com</u>
for support and guidance.

Please answer the following questions. Challenging yourself to answer the "why" after each question will give you the justification to continue that behavior...or choose to change.

- Are you living the life of your dreams? Why or why not?

- What would the life of your dreams look like? Why?

- How would you envision the life of your dreams? Why?

- Do you love your job, your business, your career? Why?

- Who are you spending your time with? Why or why not?

- Do you spend time with people that support and encourage you? Why or why not?

- Do you spend time with people who are positive and fun? Why or why not?

- How much time do you spend with your family or loved ones on a daily basis? Why or why not?

- How is your health? Why?

- How long do you want to live? Why?

- Do you eat a healthy diet and exercise regularly? Why or why not?

- How are your relationships? Why?

- Are your relationships loving and supportive or filled with anxiety and stress? Why?

- When was the last time you gave your spouse or significant other a compliment, flowers or a gift for no reason? Why or why not?

- How is your faith? Why?

- Do you believe yourself capable of achieving great things? Why or why not?

- What do you value most in your life? Why?

Chapter Two
Your Health and Longevity

"As I see it, every day you do one of two things:
build health or produce disease in yourself."
Adelle Davis (1904-1974)
American health pioneer

How is your health? Do you have enough energy to do the things you want to do? Can you walk up three flights of steps without being out of breath? Do you exercise regularly (five times per week)? Do you eat a balanced diet? Can you run around with your kids for hours and play with them at their pace? Or, are you a heart attack waiting to happen?

The most important thing you have in life is your body and its health. If you do not take great care of your body and your health, everything else will start to deteriorate around you. There is a great line in a Jimmy Buffet song called "Fruitcakes"© that goes like this, "…I treat my body like a temple, you treat yours like a tent…"

So, which one is it for you? Is it a temple or a tent? Your health, your vibrant health, is the most important tool you have that will allow you the opportunity to experience true success and create the life of your dreams.

You can have great relationships, earn a ton of money, travel the world, love your family and even be famous; however, if you drop dead at 50 because of a heart attack from never taking care of yourself, then all of the accomplishments would immediately lose all value and meaning!

Getting and staying truly healthy is a combination of many factors that **you** have control over, including:

- A clear set of goals for all areas of your life
- A good exercise regime that includes weight training, cardio training and stretching
- Drinking enough water daily
- A balanced diet of whole natural foods
- Six-eight hours of sleep per night
- Leisure activities that bring you joy--gardening, golfing, or just sitting and talking with friends

How are you doing in the areas listed above? An honest answer to this question is your first step to improving your well-being. If you are in top physical condition you can be more productive in every area of your life. Exercise alone will raise your mental alertness and give you more energy. In this chapter, I will flush out all of the chatter you hear about exercise and good health and give you solid facts, proven ideas, and some of my own anecdotes to get you headed in the right direction.

How Long Do You Want to Live?

"How long do you want to live?" To my amazement I have found that most people have never asked themselves this question. They have set goals for their relationships, finances, travel and careers, but they have never thought about how long they want to live. Knowing how long you want to live will help you change what you do and how you act today, tomorrow, and next week. Your mind will start to shift and things that once seemed unimportant, like your health, all of a sudden become critical.

- How long do you want to live?
- Why do you want to live that long?
- How are you going to live that long?

The answers to these three critical questions will change your life and how you look at your health forever.

My personal experience in observing someone who never answered these questions involved my own mother. I don't think she ever thought about how long she wanted to live. If she had answered this question, she would have surely changed her lifestyle. My father, on the other hand, lived until he was 80. For some people, 80 sounds like a great number and a ripe old age. I feel differently.

For me, 80 years old is not long enough. *My goal is to live to be 100, and there are many reasons for this:* I want to see my descendants experience as much joy as possible, I want to have as much time on this earth to experience as many things as I can with my family, I want to see my grandkids and great-grandkids, I want to teach my grandchildren how to surf and golf and I want to take them fishing. At 100, my daughter Bayley will be 72, Ellie will be 70, Jack will be 67, Benjamin will be 64 and my wife Carrie will be 100 as well. Now that sounds fun to me! Best of all, this means I have many, many years left to enjoy. Now this may seem like a lofty goal but I want to give myself every chance I can to live this long. To attempt this, I must exercise, eat right and have a clear mental picture of where I want to go and what I want to be. It will take discipline and good decisions, medical treatments and maybe a cane or a walker! But whatever it takes, I will do my best to make it to 100.

If you also think living to 100 sounds enticing, I recommend a book called *The Blue Zones*, by Dan Buettner, www.bluezones.com. In this book, Dan studies the four places in the world where the greatest concentration of centenarians (people who live to be 100) live. He talks about their lifestyle, exercise habits, and diet. It is a fun read and extremely informative.

In the following section, I will discuss what I call **The Four Components of Health**™. These are comprised of what I believe to be the four most important topics that control your health and, in turn, affect your longevity. What I provide in this section is not medical advice, but more of a common sense approach to living a healthy lifestyle. I have managed to condense what is sometimes hundreds of pages of information into only 22 pages, provide enough detail to get you started down the right path and keep it simple enough to understand.

The Four Components of Health™

1. **Heredity**
2. **How You Think and Act**
3. **What You Eat**
4. **How You Exercise**

1. Heredity

Your heredity is the one component of health that you cannot control. You are what you are and there is nothing you can do about this—you have to decide to work with and be grateful for what you were given at birth as it pertains to your body and the lineage that is passed to you by both your mother and father. Know your family's (health) history and background. Make sure you understand the pros and cons of your heredity. You must be aware of the health risks of your immediate and extended family and do what you can to guard against them.

2. How You Think and Act

This is very critical. At an early age you are conditioned to think a certain way about life, money, health, how you eat, what you eat and what relationships mean; however, as an adult you have complete control over your thoughts and ideas. Think about what you were taught as a child regarding diet, health and exercise. In hindsight, was it beneficial or harmful? Some of us were taught to eat fried food and to always clean our plate. Others were taught to eat fresh fruits and vegetables and to stop eating when we were full. In some families, smoking was shunned and forbidden; in others, everyone smoked and it was perfectly acceptable.

In the next two sections I will discuss what I call the **Extra Year Eliminators**™ and the **Extra Year Extenders**™. Both of these concepts will play into how you currently think and act about life and your health. As you read these, think about some of the risks currently present in your life and what you can do to turn these around. At the same time, think about some of the things you are doing right and how you can strive to do more of them.

Extra Year Eliminators™

"Extra years" are any years you are alive beyond the average life expectancy for a male (73) and a female (77). **Extra Year Eliminators™** are the things you are doing that may take years off of your life. Below is a list of the top risk factors:

Being Overweight

If you are 20, 30 or 40 pounds overweight, **you are taking years off of your life.** If you are 30 pounds overweight you are taking an average of seven years off of your life. Being overweight can cause an increased risk of heart disease, stroke, Type 2 diabetes, colon, gall bladder, prostate and kidney cancer, breathing problems, arthritis, immobility, gout and sleep apnea. Currently, statistics show that there are 60 million overweight people in America—that is 1 in 5 people. Simply dropping 10-20 pounds over the course of a year can add years to your life, relieve stress on joints, and provide you with more energy than you can imagine.

Smoking

If you smoke daily you are going to take an average of ten years off of your life. Smoking is one of the biggest risk factors to your health. It can cause cancer, emphysema, and shortness of breath. If you currently smoke, find a program that can assist you in stopping as soon as you can.

Sedentary Lifestyle

Those who have a sedentary lifestyle are more likely to be overweight. People with a sedentary lifestyle tend to suffer from a myriad of bad health conditions that usually include obesity, poor diet, and tobacco use.

No Goals, No Direction, No Plan

Someone who does not have health goals or a clear vision of where they are going is putting themselves at risk. If you do not know where you are going, you will get lost! If you have no plan for what to eat, how to exercise, or how to improve your health, you are at risk. Similarly, you must have goals, direction and a plan for what you want your weight, blood pressure, and cholesterol to be. You must have a clear mental picture of what good health means. I will cover goal setting in detail in Chapter 6 and I suggest you start with your health goals.

Stress

Stress affects us in many different ways. All stress is not bad, but too much stress of any kind can take years off of your life. Stress can come from many sources, such as finances, co-workers, family, traffic and information overload (the internet, email, cell phones). You must evaluate the source of your stress and determine if it is coming from things you can or cannot control. You need a **mental plan** to deal with the stress. For example, if your stress is caused by sitting in traffic during your commute, think about an alternative schedule or mode of transportation. If it is financial stress - not enough money - again you need a plan that would allow you to earn more income or spend less of what you earn or both. You also need a **physical plan** to handle stress. For me, it is working out. Exercise lowers my stress level and always makes me feel better. Find that key thing or combination of activities that allows you a complete escape from the stresses in your life. Working out or running, going to the movies, gardening, or reading are different ways many people combat stress.

Give yourself an honest evaluation based on the above information. Are you at risk from any of the factors above? What can you do to eliminate these risks?

Extra Year Extenders™

The Extra Year Extenders™ will enhance your current health and allow you to literally add extra years to your life. They are not hard--in some cases they are slight changes in your lifestyle. The benefit is a longer, healthier life and more years to enjoy whatever it is you love doing!

Exercise

Exercise is the most important factor in extending your life. Regular exercise, performed for 30-60 minutes, five days per week will assist in limiting your risk of obesity, osteoporosis, heart disease and many other possible ailments. Exercise stimulates your brain, heart, other vital organs and it elevates your endorphin levels, which gives you a sense of euphoria, also known as "runners high."

Diet of Whole Natural Foods

Choosing a diet filled with whole natural foods is the second best thing you can do to extend your life. Whole natural foods consist of fresh fruits, fresh vegetables, grains, pasta, cereal and eggs. Whole natural foods are as close to their original state as possible--the fresher and more colorful the better. Choose lean cuts of beef and chicken that are organic, free range and raised without growth hormones. We will discuss diet in more detail later in this chapter. If it is wrapped in cellophane **don't eat it!** Most of this food is highly processed and full of additives and preservatives.

Reduce Stress

Regular exercise will reduce stress. Another way to decrease stress is to control technology. Try putting all electronics on silent mode and disable the notification alerts for emails that dump into your computer, BlackBerry, or i-Phone. Check them at your convenience. Get organized and eliminate stacks of paper—make time each day (15-30 minutes) to do this. Give away the belongings you do not need or use on a regular basis and reduce clutter.

Developing Great Relationships

Positive and productive relationships enhance and lengthen your life. A loving spouse and good relationships with your family, friends, and colleagues will help you maintain purpose in life and bring laughter into it as well. Relationships give us a sense of belonging and purpose in life, especially as we grow older. Set up a date to have dinner with people you enjoy. Make time each week for those you adore.

3. <u>What You Eat</u>

For many of us, what and how we eat today is a direct reflection of how we were raised and what we were taught about food. If you were taught good habits, hold onto them and continue to find ways to improve your diet and choices of foods you consume. If you learned bad habits or incorrect information, you will need to re-educate yourself about the good and bad foods and how they affect your body. Let the following be your guide:

<u>The Power Foods</u>™

These are foods that you should eat on a regular basis. Try to choose whole natural foods and use this easy rule: think color. Red, yellow, dark green, blue, and purple--all of these colored foods are packed with the nutrients, vitamins and antioxidants your body needs.

- Salmon (one or two times per week)
- Blueberries, raspberries, strawberries, apples and citrus (daily)
- Green, yellow, orange and red peppers (daily)
- Flaxseed oil and olive oil (daily)
- Nuts—almonds and walnuts are the best (daily)

- Spinach, dark leaf lettuce, broccoli and wheat grass (daily)
- Sweet potatoes, brown rice, grains (daily)
- High fiber cereal--Kashi, Total and Raisin Bran are some of the best (daily)
- Black beans, kidney beans, garbanzo beans (daily)
- Soy milk or hemp milk (daily)
- Lean meats—chicken, lean beef, lean pork (limit to 5-6 times per week)
- Green tea (daily)
- 8-10 glasses of water (daily)

Buy the majority of your foods and groceries from the produce section, nothing from the frozen section, and nothing from the snacks and cookie aisle! Eat foods that are as close to their natural state as possible!

The Empty Foods™

These are foods that should be limited to one-two times per week or completely eliminated if possible. I like to enjoy some good ice cream, chips, or a doughnut every now and then, but I just don't make it a daily habit. Completely avoid anything with high fructose corn syrup or partially-hydrogenated oil. These two ingredients are typically found in highly processed foods that provide little nutritional value and are packed with calories and saturated fat. Just look at the ingredients on a can of Crisco--it has one ingredient and that is partially hydrogenated oil. It was created in a lab to improve the shelf life of food and it is awful for you.

Check labels when you are shopping and you will be amazed at how many products have these two ingredients. You should also avoid soda. Sodas are packed with sugar, and if they are diet sodas they are also packed with chemicals. If you are going to drink carbonated beverages, limit yourself to just three or four 12oz. servings per week. Also limit or avoid white sugar and white flour. Both are void of any true benefit to the body and cause unnecessary weight gain when consumed too often.

Avoid or limit the following:

- Soda
- White bread
- Fast food
- Butter substitutes and spreads
- Frozen foods (that include ingredients and chemicals that you cannot pronounce)
- Pastries, cookies, bagels, crackers
- Candy
- Anything wrapped in cellophane (I included this twice in this chapter on purpose)
- Processed cheese (jarred or soft blocks)
- Anything with partially hydrogenated oils (also known as trans-fats), high fructose corn syrup, powdered eggs, powdered milk, and store-bought cookies and cakes wrapped in cellophane

When shopping always look at food labels. Look for items with natural ingredients that you can pronounce. Always remember, the fewer the number of ingredients the better. Our access to unhealthy food is overwhelming, with convenience stores, and fast food restaurants located on nearly every street corner. They serve cheap, unhealthy food that can cause health risks to millions of people world-wide. Do not make stops at these types of establishments part of your routine.

Natural Health Remedies and Enhancers

I am not a big fan of prescription drugs or medications. They have their place in our society, but I stay away from them unless it involves a serious situation. I have discovered some natural remedies and supplements that provide health benefits naturally and work with the body's natural flow.

- **Powdered greens**
  I recommend Catie's Greens© or Pure Energy Greens with MSM© from Anthony Robbins. These are easy to drink and provide the following benefits: emulsification of bad cholesterol and fat, increased energy & stamina, bolsters the immune system, removes heavy metals, increases circulation, and balances pH levels.

- **Braggs Raw Unfiltered Apple Cider Vinegar**
  Mix two teaspoons with 4-6 ounces of water and drink one-two times per day. Improves digestion, balances pH levels, prevents heartburn and lowers cholesterol levels.

- **Cholestene - red yeast rice**
  Red yeast rice has become the most popular and, for many, the most effective over-the-counter op-

tion for cholesterol control. Red yeast rice is the active ingredient in Cholestene©. This product produces healthy cholesterol levels.

- **Res-Q 1250 fish oil supplement**
Res-Q 1250 provides an essential balance of the specific omega-3s, EPA and DHA, which optimize cardiovascular health, encourage the reduction of inflammation within the body, reduce the amount of triglycerides in your blood and help blood fats (lipids) stay suspended in the blood instead of sticking to the inside of the arteries.

- **Hemp milk** – One eight-ounce glass contains 800 mg Omega-3 with SDA, 2600 mg of Omega-6 with GLA, all 10 essential amino acids, 4 grams digestible protein, vitamins A, B12, D, E, riboflavin & folic acid, magnesium, potassium, phosphorus, iron & zinc, and provides 40% daily value of calcium.

Using the products listed above, along with a balanced diet and regular exercise, I was able to reduce my cholesterol from a high of 277 down to 217. I do not currently use a cholesterol-lowering drug and probably never will. All of these products have tremendous health benefits, typically have no side effects, and are 100% natural. Links for all of these products can be found on the resource page of our web site www.thepracticalguidetoexceptionalliving.com/resources.

Be Mindful of How Much You Eat

As Americans, the amount of food we are served and consume on a daily basis is absurd. The average American should consume about 2000 calories per day. (If you work out regularly, this could be as high as 3000 calories per day). The problem we run into is two-fold:

– The portions we are served in restaurants and at home are huge and often enough for two or three people.
– We have been taught to finish what is on our plate.

Considering these factors, it is no wonder we have an obesity epidemic in America. You must do your best to fight against these elements. Here are some helpful tips:

- When eating out, go to French, café style restaurants or tapas bars that serve smaller portions
- Order the smallest size of whatever you can
- When eating fast food order a child's meal
- **Never super size anything!**
- At restaurants, eat half of your meal and save the leftovers for another meal or give the food to someone in need
- Never let yourself get famished--always have a healthy snack available
- Eat slowly and completely chew your food completely before taking another bite
- Practice leaving a little food on your plate after each meal (my mother-in-law lives by this!)

- Drink two big glasses of water first thing in the morning
- Eat breakfast every day
- Eat six small meals per day
- A maximum serving size of a carbohydrate, vegetable, or protein is the size of a clenched fist

4. How You Exercise

I have mentioned several times in this book that exercise is the most important factor in improving and maintaining your overall health. What most people get confused about is the difference between exercise time and exercise intensity. You can exercise for two hours at a very slow, walking pace and not get the benefits you could achieve from 30 minutes of heart- pounding, vigorous exercise. It is all about the burn rate. How many calories are you going to burn while you exercise, and how many calories will you continue to burn when you stop? I mix up the types of workouts I do almost daily to avoid repetitive motions. My goal is to burn as many calories as I can in as little time as possible. Here are my suggestions for an effective exercise program:

(Consult your doctor and a professional trainer before starting any exercise regimen, especially if you have not exercised for a long time.)

- 30-60 minutes per day of vigorous exercise at least five days per week
- Variety in any exercise program is essential--include biking, running, elliptical training, weight-lifting, yoga, swimming and stretching

- Get your heart rate up to the 65-85% range and keep it there for the duration of your exercise (Invest in an inexpensive heart rate monitor)
- Burn 500-1000 calories per hour
- Cross-train with 30 minutes of weight training combined with 30 minutes of cardio
- Do ab exercises and use exercise balls
- Stretching prevents soreness and injury--flexibility decreases as we age, so make sure to stretch at least 10-15 minutes per day before and after exercising

There are thousands of books, tapes and seminars about how to exercise, how to get six- pack abs, how to firm your butt and how to tone your hips, arms and thighs. At the end of the day, it all comes down to you. **How hard, how long, and how often are you willing to work out?** If you go to the gym and walk for 45 minutes, at least you are doing something. But, if you go to the gym and lift hard for 20 minutes and then run hard for 20 minutes, the benefits to your body and the calories you burn will be so much greater. One of the best books on this subject is *Body for Life* by Bill Phillips. Bill explains why it is not so much how long you work out, but the intensity at which you work out that really counts.

Constant Movement Exercise™

I have developed a concept that I call **Constant Movement Exercise™**. The key is you never allow your body to stop moving from the time you start your work out until it ends. There is no pausing in between sets, not even taking a break to walk to the water fountain. You constantly move from one exercise to the next, keeping up the intensity every step of the way. **CME**™ incorporates weight training, core exercises, circuit training, stationary bike, elliptical training and floor exercises into a 60-minute workout that never stops.

The main point of this chapter is the importance of your health as it pertains to producing an exceptional life. With great health, all of your other dreams become more possible and your chances of seeing them to fruition and being here to enjoy them are greatly increased. Take time to think about your current health and what you may need to do to improve your lifestyle. To your longevity!

Chapter Two Summary
Your Health and Longevity

Key Points to Remember

- You must have a goal for how long you want to live and describe why you want to live this long

- You must have goals for your diet, exercise program, weight, cholesterol and blood pressure

- Drink eight-ten glasses of water daily

- Sleep six-eight hours per night

- Stop any behavior that falls under Extra Year Eliminators™ such as being overweight, smoking and having a sedentary or stressful lifestyle

- Study and engage in activities that are included in the Extra Year Extenders™ such as regular exercise, diet of whole natural foods, reduction of stress and cultivating strong relationships

- Understand the history of your family's health risks (heredity)

- Be careful about how you think or have been taught to think about your health, diet and exercise

- Study the Power Foods™ and their importance in your everyday diet

- Study the Empty Foods™ and eliminate or limit them in your daily diet

- Eat six small meals per day and never super-size anything!

- Exercise 30-60 minutes at least five days per week

- Variety is the key to a successful exercise program--use cardio, weight training, yoga, swimming, biking and running

- Try to use natural supplements in place of prescription drugs whenever possible

Go to
www.thepracticalguidetoexceptionalliving.com
for support and guidance.

Please answer the following questions. Challenging yourself to answer the "why" after each question will give you the justification to continue that behavior...or choose to change.

- How long do you want to live? Why?

- How will you live this long? Why?

- Do you eat a healthy diet and exercise regularly? Why or why not?

- What changes in your lifestyle do you need to make? Why?

- What Extra Year Eliminators™ do you need to stop or control? Why?

- What Extra Year Extenders™ do you need to start or continue? Why?

- How can you reduce your stress? Why?

- What were you taught about health as a child?

- Was your family's lifestyle healthy or unhealthy? How?

- Do you have a family history of heart disease, cancer, obesity, and alcohol or drug abuse?

- What have you done as an adult to improve your health?

- Do you believe you can attain the weight you want?

- What is your health plan?

- What Power Foods™ do you currently eat on a regular basis? Why?

- What Empty Foods™ do you currently eat on a regular basis? Why?

- What is your ideal weight? Why?

- What are your health goals for the next 30-60-90-180 days? Why?

Chapter Three
The Power of Gratitude and Faith

*"Gratitude unlocks the fullness of life. It turns what
we have into enough, and more. It turns denial into
acceptance, chaos into order, and confusion into clarity...
it turns problems into gifts, failures into success, the
unexpected into perfect timing, and mistakes into
important events. Gratitude makes sense of our past,
brings peace for today and creates a vision for tomorrow."*
Melody Beatty (1948-)
Author, Journalist, Teleplay Writer

Are you grateful for the life that you have? Are you grateful to live in this great country we call America? **Gratitude - being truly grateful - is the most powerful emotion we possess.** The only way to move forward and design the life of your dreams is to be truly grateful, right now, in this moment, for all that you have. Showing gratitude, no matter what your situation, is the **key** that will unlock the door to future fulfillment.

If you are anything like me, you may have the same reaction I had when I first contemplated this. I thought of all the problems I had in my life. I was battling a lawsuit, working myself to death and not making enough money. I thought about these circumstances and wondered, how am I supposed to feel grateful? So I began praying in earnest to find the strength and the reasons to feel grateful. And as I sat there praying, I realized that although I had difficult situations in my life, I also had this: a beautiful, loving, caring and supportive wife, four beautiful children, supportive friends, family, money in reserve, a roof over my head, God and a church that supported me, a great lawyer…and the list went on. The list rejuvenated me. This is what is called my Gratitude List. I never stray too far from that list because I know that any obstacle can be overcome by simply feeling grateful.

I learned a lot about gratitude from *The Secret* by Rhonda Byrne www.thesecret.tv. Rhonda speaks about the power of gratitude. She makes it a habit to say thank you hundreds of times every day. From the moment she wakes up until she goes to bed at night, she is saying thank you and being grateful for every minute of every day. I have adopted this ritual and it has done wonders for me and those around me. I say "thank you" for everything - the beautiful day, the sunshine, warmth, the rain, challenges that allow me to learn, for my triumphs and all of the joys that make life this wonderful experience. I say thank you all the time. If you adopt this ritual as well you will start to realize how good it makes you feel. So often people will start the day on the wrong track and it will stick with them all day. Try this in the morning instead!

The Gratitude List

A Gratitude List is an easy way to capture all of the things that make you feel grateful. It makes you instantly realize all of the blessings in your life and immediately elevates your mental state. Make a Gratitude List now:

- Take a clean sheet of paper
- Set a timer for five minutes
- Write down as quickly as you can all of the things you are grateful for in short, one to two word blasts
- Start with, "I am thankful to be alive"
- List friends, family members, challenges you have overcome, triumphs you have had, goals you have reached, your health
- When the timer goes off, go back and write down all of the reasons you are so grateful for these things
- Write the top ten things you are grateful for on a 3x5 index card and carry it with you for the rest of your life
- Update this list on your birthday every year, or as often as you like

Your mental state will completely shift when you see how many things you have in your life that make you feel grateful. In order for you to move forward in life you must be grateful for all that you have at this moment.

Faith

What does the word faith mean to you? Do you have faith in your own abilities? Do you have confidence in others?

Having faith means more than just a relationship with God. For me, I have found that having faith means getting up every day and knowing that the day will go well. Having faith means knowing your kids will make the right decisions in life and on a daily basis. Having faith means supporting your loved ones when they have made a big mistake or are being challenged emotionally. Faith is more than religion. You must know and trust deep in your soul, life is going to be good to you and to those around you. Faith is knowing that when you are faced with challenges, you will get through them and become a better person through the adversity. True faith is believing in everything you spend your time doing.

Faith in Yourself

Faith must start with a belief in you. **You have to have faith in yourself first, and then you can face whatever challenges you may encounter**. This means you must be honest with yourself and honest about what is going on in your life. If you believe in yourself and are true to yourself, you can accomplish anything. This does not mean you will always succeed, but it does mean that you have enough certitude in yourself and in your ideas that you will always give 100% and put your best foot forward. Remember, feeling good about yourself starts with confidence in both physical and mental health. If you are taking great care of your body, you will look good, feel good and in turn you will have more faith in yourself and your self esteem will soar.

Faith in Others

You must also have faith in your loved ones and those you associate with on a regular basis. Most of all have faith in your spouse. This is the person you have made a commitment to for a lifetime. You must believe in him/her and you need to give him/her a million reasons every day to believe in you. You must have faith in your friends. You must have faith and trust in business associates. These are some of the most important people in your life and you have to be confident that they are going to make good decisions and be honest in their transactions.

Faith in Society

You must also have faith in others and in society as a whole. I have great trust in our government and the freedom and democracy it provides. Have faith in your neighbor and your community. Have belief in your fellow human beings and understand that most people want the same things you want: love, food, shelter, recognition and acceptance. We should all want the best for our fellow man.

Showing gratitude for what you have and where you are and having faith in yourself and your fellow man will erase the most damaging emotion of all: pessimism. **Pessimism and negative attitudes cannot survive where true gratitude and faith reside.**

A Spiritual Awakening

Have you ever had a moment when you felt the presence of God?

Although I have always believed in a higher power or something bigger than us, I never used to really feel a true connection to God. I went to church as a youth and to Sunday school, but that was about it. Religion and a true belief in God were subjects that I felt uncomfortable discussing. Only the religious "weirdoes" openly talked about their faith and belief in God. Luckily for me, that has all changed.

The first time I felt a true connection to God and began to understand the impact this can have on your life was when my first child was born. Watching my children come into this world was the most amazing thing I had ever experienced. In fact, nothing has even come close. To think that the love of two people could create such an amazing result was beyond explanation. This is when Carrie and I starting thinking more about God and our faith. At the time, it was on more of a subconscious level, something we could not easily explain. What I have found is that discovering a connection with God is not necessarily an event, it is a journey. It is a journey of discovery that never ends.

My next experience occurred just before Christmas 2006. My business was barely making a profit, I was embroiled in a lawsuit that had cost me over $100,000, and I was being evicted from three different office locations as a result of the lawsuit. I was deflated, exhausted and humiliated. Late one night, when I could not sleep, I was sitting at my computer, staring at the screen. I got up and walked into our family room. I got on my knees and I started to cry. I also began to pray.

"God, why are you letting this happen to me? I am a good guy, I work hard, I take care of my family, I am a loving husband, father, and friend, I go to church, I give to the church, I pay my taxes, how can you let this happen to me?" To my surprise a response came back to me. It said *"You are doing this to yourself. It's your negative attitude and the fact that you are feeling sorry for yourself."* I sat in silence for a while and thought about this. I replied out loud, *"OK, you are right, so from now on I will be positive and I will take full responsibility for whatever happens in my life, but I cannot do this on my own. Moving forward, God, we are partners. You help me get the right people on board, get me through this lawsuit, and from now on I have you on my team to help me with my business, my relationships, my family, and my life, and we can share all of the challenges, triumphs and fun together."*

That was it, word for word. And my life was changed forever.

The results I have experienced in my life and with my business have completely changed since that night. My business is very profitable, the team we have at my company Sharp Details, Inc. is the strongest and the best in the industry, my patience has grown tremendously, my tolerance level for things that used to send me through the roof has greatly improved, the time I have for my family has increased ten-fold, my health is vibrant and my relationships are stronger than ever. My relationship with God has grown and developed into something that is a pillar in my life. When you know that everything you do is being done with the help of God, the burden and stress become so much lighter and your confidence in yourself and in your abilities soars.

I encourage you to try to forge a relationship with God, whatever that means to you. It will feel uncomfortable at first, but trust me: it gets easier as you go along. I also recommend you get a book by Neale Donald Walsch called *Conversations with God* www.nealedonaldwalsch.com. Walsch gives you a sense of the sort of open and honest discussions you can have with God.

The Earpiece Conversation™

This is a technique I developed and use almost daily. It gives me the opportunity to talk with God in my car, when I am alone. I call it the **Earpiece Conversation™**. I simply put in my phone earpiece and have a conversation with God. I always start with thanking him for all that I have in my life or for whatever small triumph I have had that day. Often I thank him for giving me patience as I sit in traffic! My earpiece is always in so people think I am on the phone and not crazy. Give it a try.

Finding a Place of Worship

For my family, finding a place of worship was a spiritual journey. We had moved back to Alexandria, Virginia after being away for several years. We visited many churches and never felt a strong connection to any of them. Sometimes it was the sermon, sometimes the time of the service did not work for us and sometimes it was the Sunday school for the kids. We just could not find the one that *felt* right. I will repeat this--we just could not find the church that *felt* right.

This was extremely important for us. We knew we had to keep looking. My wife wanted to attend a service at St. John's Church in Washington D.C. St. John's is known as "The Church of the Presidents." It is a beautiful, old church that was built in 1815 and is located across from the White House at 16th and H Streets in Lafayette Square. St. John's is about a 20-30 minute drive from our house in Alexandria. This is not exactly my idea of a relaxing, Sunday morning drive with four kids!

But I relented and we attended St. John's one Sunday. And I am grateful to say that we found the right place of worship for our family that day. It was a beautiful summer day and when we walked up to the church, almost instantly it just *felt* right. The clergy were very welcoming and it seemed as if we had known them for years. The sermon given by the Reverend Luis Leon was wonderful, and Carrie and I both commented on how we felt a connection with his message. The kids went to Sunday school and enjoyed their teachers and their classmates. As we exited the church that day, the assistant rector, Peter, took an extra moment with us and asked us a few questions. He engaged each of the kids and thanked us several times for coming to St. John's. As we drove home we all agreed that this church deserved a second visit. A few days later a handwritten note arrived at our house from Peter. In it, he thanked Carrie, me, and our children by name for attending the service and requested that we come back again to get to know the church a little better. Being a businessperson in charge of sales and marketing for my own company, I was sold. We began attending regularly and now consider this church part of our family.

Luis Leon has also become a special person in our life. He has a knack for delivering a sermon that hits the nail on the head every time. It is always a blend of Biblical, reality, and spirituality and always spiked with a little humor. The most important thing for me is that he urges me to think about and take stock in the direction of my life. He makes me pause and think about my faith and how I am serving God. His sermons always make me feel as if he is talking directly to me--like he knows me intimately and has been in the trunk of my car all week! Luis has not only become a special person to Carrie and me but also to our children. They adore him. Knowing him as a pastor and a friend has improved our lives.

We searched and searched until we found St. John's Church, and we chose it because we felt connected to it. St. John's Church feeds us, and in turn we always feel grateful, hopeful, challenged, and alive and rejuvenated when we go! I beg you to find a place of worship that you love.

Chapter Three Summary
The Power of Gratitude and Faith

Key Points to Remember

- You must be grateful today for all of the blessings you have in your life

- After love, gratitude is the most powerful emotion we have

- Being grateful for what you have right now will give you the power and faith to move onto bigger and better things

- Say thank you every day and often for all of the gifts and blessings you have

- Make a Gratitude List--look at it and update it often

- Have faith in yourself and have faith in your ideas

- Have faith in God, your country, your neighbor, your family and your friends

- Find a connection to God in your life and you will be amazed at how it changes your life

- Talk to God and ask for help with all that ails you

- Ask God to be your partner in your life, your business and your relationships

- Find a way to make church and faith an important part of your life

- Find the right church for you!

- Find a church that makes you feel energized and excited!

- Seek out what God, faith and belief mean to you and discover the difference it can make in your life

Please answer the following questions. Challenging yourself to answer the "why" after each question will give you the justification to continue that behavior...or choose to change.

- Do you act grateful for what you have today? Why or why not?

- What are you grateful for? Why?

- Do you have a Gratitude List? Why or why not?

- What does the word faith mean to you? Why?

- Do you have faith in yourself and your abilities? Why or why not?

- Do you have faith in others? Why or why not?

- Do you have a relationship with God? Why or why not?

- Do you have faith in your community and country? Why or why not?

- Have you ever had a moment when you truly felt the presence of God? How?

- Do you feel comfortable talking to God? Why or why not?

- Do you go to church on a regular basis? Why or why not?

- Do you enjoy the church you attend? Why or why not?

- How do you feel when you attend church? Why?

- Do you think faith and belief should be important to you? Why or why not?

Chapter Four
Attitude and the Law of Attraction

"If you think you can or you think you can't, you are probably right."
Henry Ford (1863-1947)
Founder, Ford Motor Company

Your attitude will determine your destiny. Attitude is everything. With the right attitude and the right frame of mind, anything can be accomplished. You must have a positive attitude and be optimistic about your prospects in life, the world we live in and the people around us. Does this describe you? Are you generally positive? Or are you generally negative... about your family, your job and the world around you? An honest evaluation about your attitude could make the difference between a life that is truly abundant (positive) or a life that never delivers (negative).

A Negative Attitude

A negative attitude: this one trait keeps people from achieving great things in life and they don't even know it. A pessimistic person is someone who always looks at life as though it is some kind of hell they have been forced to endure. This is someone who always looks at the down side of everything: it is too hot or too cold, too sunny, or too rainy. In families, a mother or father with a negative attitude will project this view of life to their children and a terrible cycle of negativity will continue. In a company, a person with a negative attitude can become a cancer that sickens all those around him or her. The expression "one bad apple can ruin the barrel" could not be truer. One negative person can affect your team, your department, your customers and a whole company if this person stays around too long.

There are a lot of people out there that spend much of their energy gossiping, talking ill of others, or being negative. I call these people "**energy drains.**" If you know someone who is an **energy drain,** avoid them at all costs. If you must spend time with them, always limit it and make sure to give yourself a good dose of positive thought before and after you spend time with them.

A Positive Attitude

A positive attitude: this one trait allows people to achieve great things in life, and they know it. A positive person looks at life as an exciting journey they have been given the privilege to enjoy. This is someone who always looks at the up-side of everything: the cold is a nice break from the heat, the heat feels great, the plants need the rain and the wind makes for a perfect day to fly a kite. The positive person never lets the weather affect their attitude. It is easy to spot such a person. They walk around with their head held high, they look straight ahead and smile to others, they walk briskly like they have somewhere to go and there is a spring in their step. If you say "hi" to this person, they smile and say "hi" in return. If you ask, "how are you doing" they will respond with the following answers: great, awesome, wonderful, or they will start to explain to you in detail all of the things that are right and just with the government, their neighbor, their spouse, religion, and the world. In families, a mother or father with a positive attitude will project this view of life to their children and a wonderful cycle of optimism will continue. In a company, a person with a positive attitude can become a force that can rejuvenate all of those around him or her. The expression, "One positive, optimistic leader could right the ship" rings very true. One positive person onboard can improve your team, your department, your customer loyalty and a whole company. A positive attitude can be taught and learned. It takes discipline and time.

How would you fit into the paragraphs above? Do you consider yourself positive or negative? Here are five things you can do to feel positive immediately (do these often):

1) Make a Gratitude List (Chapter 3) and read it often.

2) Whenever you talk to someone, in person or on the phone, smile—it will project a positive attitude.

3) Pray for a positive attitude and for ways to look at the world in a positive light.

4) In every situation, ask "What is good here? What can I learn? How can I help?"

5) Also, ask yourself, "If everyone did what I am doing, would the world be better or worse off?"

You must convince yourself that every situation in life has an up-side—an opportunity to learn something about others and ourselves. Often, it is in the face of our greatest adversity that we find our greatest achievement.

Laugh, Laugh, Laugh

The Norman Cousins Story

Norman Cousins was a prominent political journalist, author, professor and world peace advocate. As Norman aged he found out he had a severe case of heart disease. He was told he might not recover and that he would have to stay in the hospital for some time. Not liking what he heard, he decided to develop his own process to get better.

He fought back against the disease by taking massive doses of Vitamin C and, according to his book, by training himself to laugh. He would get Marx Brothers movies and other films filled with humor and he would watch them to make himself laugh. Those 10 minutes of laughter had an anesthetic affect and would give him at least two hours of pain-free sleep. When the painkilling effect of the laughter wore off, he would switch on the motion picture projector again, which would lead to another pain-free interval. Norman Cousins realized the power of laughter, and he used it to help recover.

This is one of the most extraordinary examples of laughter being used as medicine. We have all heard the expression "Laughter is the best medicine."

Laughter can be used as a self-medicating trigger in various situations. Laughter can help you feel better when you are feeling down. Laughter can help you communicate with others. Laughter can break the ice when you first meet someone or are giving a speech.

I used laughter and humor when I had to give the eulogy at my father's funeral, which was very difficult for me to do. Knowing I would struggle to get through the eulogy, my brother, Joe, developed a sign he would give me if I started to get choked up. He sat in the front row and every time I paused or started to get emotional, he would flash me the sign. It was hilarious and it provided humor, not only for me, but for our wives who were sitting close enough to see him do it each time. I also used humor throughout the eulogy because I didn't want people sobbing and crying at my dad's funeral - I wanted them laughing. We also spent many hours laughing at the reception as we listened to hours of stories about my dad from his best man and best friend, Jack Carney. Laughter helped ease our grief that day and allowed us to actually enjoy visiting with others.

Laugh at Yourself

One of the best ways to get through a tough time is to laugh at yourself. We must be able to find humor in the mistakes and blunders we will all make as we go through life. None of us should take ourselves so seriously that we cannot laugh at some of the things we do and say at the wrong time.

Laughter is so valuable for changing our mood and our state. What are all of the different things that make you laugh? Think of events, movies, funny phrases, or different experiences you have had in your life, with your kids, friends, family and colleagues, that immediately bring on laughter. My children Bayley, Ellie, Jack, and Benjamin have given me more to laugh and be joyful about than anything else in the world. From the time they were tiny, my children have brought tears to my eyes: watching them talk on their "foot phones," act out plays, nurse their baby dolls like mommy does and listening to them sing when they think no one is around. Our house is never quiet with four children and more often than not it is laughter that is the loudest noise and that is fine by me! As our pastor in Delaware used to say, "The sound of children laughing is a blessed noise."

The Law of Attraction

Have you ever heard of the Law of Attraction? It is a universal law, similar to the law of gravity or the law of night and day. What goes up must come down, day follows night and night follows day. These are universal laws that cannot be changed. The Law of Attraction works exactly the same way.

Every human abides by the Law of Attraction:

- **Like attracts like**
- **Positive thoughts and feelings attract positive outcomes into your life**
- **Negative thoughts and feelings attract negative things into your life**
- **As you think, you shall become**
- **What you think you deserve, good or bad, you will receive**

If you think that the world is a hard, difficult and cruel place, then as a result of this thinking, that is what your life will become. Conversely, if you view the world as being full of opportunity, abundance and joy, then, as a result of that thinking, that is what your life will become.

How you think every day will control your actions and what you do every day. This, in turn will produce results, good, bad, or indifferent.

Where you are in your life right now is where your thoughts and feelings have brought you, period. You must accept 100% responsibility for where you are right now in your journey. When I first heard this, I refused to believe it. How could my thoughts control my destiny? Look at the statement in bold above and you will find your answer. This is the key. How you think controls how you act, which determines where you end up in life. The Law of Attraction will bring to you whatever it is you think about yourself and your life each day.

Understanding and mastering the Law of Attraction have changed my life forever. Here is an example using my own inner dialogue—my thoughts about my business – and the results:

Old Thoughts, Old Results (1994-2006)

- Owning a business is hard work
- No one cares as much as I do
- I can't find good people
- Employees are the problem
- Why are customers so difficult and demanding?
- I will never find good people

- People will steal from me
- I cannot trust others
- Why is everyone out to hurt me and my business?

As a result of my thinking, I hired poor employees that would steal (vans, money, customers and other employees) and sub-par managers that blamed me for their problems. I had a business that was rife with lawsuits and unhappy internal and external customers and generated little profit. I worked all of the time, including weekends and barely took vacation. I had attracted what I was thinking. The poor results did not lie.

New Thoughts, New Results (2007-2009)

- Owning a business is a blessing and an honor
- My team cares as much as I do
- I will attract the right people at the right time
- Employees are our greatest asset and the most important part of the team
- We find good people all the time
- My customers are the best in the world and treat me with respect
- People will help me protect the business
- I can trust others to help me grow the business
- I have full support from my family, customers, managers and employees

As a result of my faith and new attitudes and thoughts, I hired an Operations Manager I could trust with all aspects of the business. We have put together an A-class management team, and those managers have hired A-class employees who help them achieve positive results.

Ninety percent of the problems we had in the past have vanished, our customers are thrilled with our service, the revenue and profit grow each year and our managers are receiving impressive bonuses. I do not work weekends or holidays and take an average of 10 weeks off per year. I have attracted this through my thoughts, actions and beliefs in what is possible for my business. The positive results tell the story.

The Law of Attraction can almost seem like magic. With the right thoughts you will bring into your life the right people, opportunities and circumstances all at the right time. This has happened to me more times than I can begin to count and continues to happen on a weekly basis.

Visualization

The next step in the Law of Attraction is learning to visualize. Have you ever thought about a person and closed your eyes so you could picture them as if they were there? Then two days later you run into them or they call. This is not by chance. This is the Law of Attraction at work. You thought about this person, then you visualized them, and then they appeared in your life.

You must set the goal of what you truly want in your life--whether it's a better job, new career, more money, the perfect mate, better friends, a better city to live in, a bigger house, more peace of mind--whatever it is you want. Think about what you want, write it down, visualize it, commit it to memory and The Law of Attraction will go to work immediately. You have to believe it with passion. You have to think about it and read about it.

You must picture what your life would be like if you achieved these different things. You have to believe it with all your heart.

The Visualization Experience™

- Think about what it is that you truly want
- Write it down in detail with a date for completion
- Write down why you want to achieve this goal
- Write down the emotions you will feel having achieved the goal
- Close your eyes and picture how you will feel and look if you achieve this goal
- Cut out pictures describing this goal or your feeling and put them in a notebook
- Look at this daily

These actions will immediately begin to set the Law of Attraction into motion and you will be on your way to achieving this goal.

Affirmations

We all use affirmations every day whether we know it or not. Affirmations are the thoughts and phrases that run through your head every day. You have to be very careful about the subconscious messages you send yourself on a daily basis. These affirmations can be positive or negative in nature. I will share several so you can figure out what message you are sending to yourself.

I start and end every day by simply saying "thank you for all that I have, my beautiful wife, my wonderful children, my family, friends, business, our church, our wonderful schools, the challenges that make me stronger and the triumphs that feel so good. Thank you for my health and thank you for making this a great day." You must be very deliberate about your self-talk. Make sure you are sending positive and upbeat messages to yourself throughout the day.

Take Action!

Many books have been written on and discuss the Law of Attraction. I truly believe this is one of the most powerful laws you can learn to bring what you want into your life. As I have explained, it has worked for me over and over throughout my life and business career, but the most important component to the Law of Attraction often gets left out--**ACTION!** You must take massive action if you want anything to happen. You cannot sit under a lotus tree with legs crossed and eyes closed and expect a new Ferrari to drop down from the sky without taking action. Remember, you must visualize what you want, picture it as if it has already occurred and then go out and do the actions necessary to make this happen. If your thinking is right you will automatically take the right action.

Overcoming Obstacles, Adversity, Failure and Naysayers

As we go through life, it doesn't matter how much you have prepared, how great your attitude is, or how much you believe in the Law of Attraction - you are always going to have obstacles, adversity, failure (a word I don't even use) and people who will try to convince you that you will not succeed. Some obstacles and setbacks will be obvious and others will sneak up on you. You will run into different problems and roadblocks throughout your life and/or business career which you will have to overcome. Whenever you are faced with an obstacle or adversity, immediately ask yourself the following questions:

- Do I have any control over this?
- What can I learn from this experience?
- What opportunity for growth exists?
- Is this a process or system problem or is this a people problem?
- How can I use this obstacle to improve a system or process?
- Is this problem caused because of poor communication?

Asking these questions will immediately get your thinking going in a direction that is constructive and positive. This will help you to not only overcome the obstacle, but also develop ways to avoid it in the future. It is also important to understand where you want to spend your energy. I have found that if the problem or circumstance is something that is completely out of my control (weather, decisions by others, customer going out of business) then I will not give it my energy or thought.

Chapter Four Summary
Attitude and the Law of Attraction

Key Points to Remember

- Your attitude will determine your destiny

- A negative attitude will keep you from reaching your highest potential no matter what your education and experience

- A positive attitude will allow you to reach your highest potential no matter what your education and experience

- Avoid those who gossip, bad mouth others and are negative--they are "energy drains"

- Pray often for a positive attitude

- Laughter is a great way to get a positive attitude and improve your outlook on life

- Spend time with others who have good attitudes and enjoy laughing

- Find ways to laugh at yourself--it will help prevent embarrassment and taking yourself too seriously

- Study and understand the Law of Attraction

- What you think about every day you will attract into your life – both good and bad, positive and negative

- Your daily thoughts will control your actions

- Visualize what you want in your life in detail--picture exactly how things would look, sound and feel

- Great successes will often occur right after a setback or challenge--never give up

- Take action! This is the most important component of the Law of Attraction

Please answer the following questions. Challenging yourself to answer the "why" after each question will give you the justification to continue that behavior...or choose to change.

- Do you consider yourself a positive or negative person? Why?

- Do you let the weather affect your mood? Why or why not?

- Do you gossip about or speak ill of others on a regular basis? Why or why not?

- Do you know people who are an "energy drain?" Why?

- If you are in a bad or negative mood, how do you change that feeling? Why?

- Do you laugh often? Why or why not?

- Can you laugh and find humor with those you are with on a daily basis? Why or why not?

- Can you laugh at yourself and your mistakes and shortcomings? Why or why not?

- Do you understand the Law of Attraction and how it works? How?

- Do you have examples of how the Law of Attraction has worked in your life? Why or why not? Or what are they?

- Do you believe your thoughts control your actions and, in turn, your results? Why or why not?

- Can you accept 100% responsibility for where you are in your life today? Why or why not?

- How do you use positive affirmations on a daily basis? Why?

- Are you comfortable using visualization as a tool to get the results and outcomes you desire? Why or why not?

- Have you ever experienced a great triumph or success after a defeat or setback?

- How can you start using these tools in your life on a daily basis?

Chapter Five
The Money Dance

"I have been poor and I have been rich.
Believe me, honey, rich is better."
Sophie Tucker (1884-1966)
Vaudeville Entertainer

The subject of money and wealth is one that makes many people feel uncomfortable. I believe money and wealth are vital components in creating the life of your dreams. We live in a day and age where virtually all transactions are made with currency. The more money you have, the more you can do, and the more you can experience, give, share, learn about the world around us and create. The first step in allowing yourself to earn more money and start to develop true, lasting wealth is to understand how you perceive money. You must understand the psychological effect money has on you. The thoughts and tools below have allowed me to better understand money, how it works and how to earn and keep more of it to produce long-term income and financial stability.

The Money Myths

What I call the "money myths" are beliefs that exist in the minds of many people in society today about money and finances and they are as follows:

- **Only educated people who attend Ivy League schools or come from wealthy families can become wealthy (millionaires).**
  I know three people, none of whom has a college education (one of them never graduated from high school) who all started their businesses from scratch and are now multi-multi millionaires. They all came from lower-to middle class families.

- **It takes money to make money.**
  When I started my business, I had no financial help and about $100 in my checking account. As I mentioned earlier, my company today generates close to $4,000,000 in annual revenue. There are endless stories of people who started with nothing, or even greatly in debt and were able to create wealth.

- **If you become rich, you will become too good for others. Rich people are greedy, rich people are snobs, rich people are selfish.**
  If you are a wonderful, loving and generous person and you become rich, you will become even more wonderful, loving and generous; however, if you are a sarcastic jackass and you become rich, chances are you will become a bigger sar-

castic jackass. It is not the money that creates the person, the person already is who they are before and after the money is earned.

Your Money Relationship™

What has been your past relationship with money? What has money represented over the course of your life? How did your parents handle money? Did you come from a family that was rich, middle-class or poor? Did you always have plenty of money growing up, or was money something that was often scarce? Did your parents come from a wealthy family or were they self-made and did it on their own? How your parents handled money has an enormous impact on how you think about money in your adult life. Often people from meager backgrounds, even pure poverty, want to become very wealthy, while others from lots of money are resentful of it or relatively indifferent to it because they spent so little time with their success-driven parents.

Do not let your past experience with money become your future - unless, of course, the experience was positive. You have the power in today's society to create your own dreams and goals and money should be part of those dreams and goals. There is no virtue in going through life in poverty or worrying about money all the time. That serves no one. You have to understand and believe that it is OK to want and to have a lot of money. It is not wrong, evil, nor unjust. I have found that as my business and personal income has grown, the opportunities for my managers and employees, has grown as well. As their level of income and incentives has improved so has the level of service we provide to our customers. It is a true cycle of financial and business success for all of the parties involved.

The Money Beliefs™

Ask yourself the following questions so you can better determine your beliefs about money:

- Do you have enough money?
- Do you have to work hard for it?
- Do you save it or do you spend it all?
- Does your money work for you?
- If you take off three weeks do you still get paid?
- Do you generate income and profit while you sleep?

The way you answered these questions may be affecting how much money you earn right now and how much of that money you actually hang on to at the end of each month. You have to get your **attitude** going in the right direction in order to have a shot at earning the income you want and the ability to create the life of your dreams.

I want you to think hard about what it is that you want financially. Many people will join a gym, buy the right clothes and map out a very strategic plan to lose 35 pounds in the next 120 days. They will work hard, follow their plan every day and succeed! Money and income goals are exactly the same. You have to know what outcome you want financially and set up a plan to achieve that outcome. You have to use the tools I gave you in Chapter 4 on Attitude and the Law of Attraction to picture exactly what it is you want and why. Why do you want financial stability, additional wealth and more income? What will you use it for? How will it change your life? How could you use your wealth to change the lives of others?

The Money Flow™

Over the last 18 years, I have gone from making $20,000 per year working two jobs to starting my own business and earning enough to be in the top 1% of all wage earners in the country. What I have learned in that time is not so much how to make money, but discovering and appreciating the need for money to flow. Money is a fluid medium that cannot be held onto or put into mason jars and buried in the backyard. Money behaves a certain way depending on how you treat it. You must treat money and the handling of money with respect and discipline.

The Money Flow Rules™:

- As I said above, you must treat your money with respect---do not waste it on "long shot" business ideas
- Find a way to put your money to work for you (maybe through investing in a business or real estate)
- Find a way to earn money while you sleep
- Start a business, so that you can take advantage of the many tax benefits of having your own company

- Be creative in looking for ways to increase your income as much as you can each year
- You must put at least 10-15% of your income into savings that should not be touched. If you cannot afford this immediately, start with 2% or 5% and work towards the larger number. The most important first step is the discipline to save something consistently every month.
- You must give some of your money away (10% or more to charities, your church or worthy cause). Again, start with a smaller percentage if that is all you can afford and work towards a larger amount.

I will explain these rules in further detail below. All of these practices will keep money flowing and that money will eventually flow back to you in greater and greater quantities. For the past three years I have followed all of these rules and my personal income and business income have increased dramatically, even during a recession.

Money must continually flow. If you are disciplined enough to keep it flowing, it will continue to come back to you. However, if you cut it off at any one spot you will break a natural pattern and the flow will slow down.

There are three avenues that money comes from:

- The money you earn
- The money you save
- The money you give away

Every one of these avenues will bring money back to you every time, as long as you believe and continue to follow these rules. Just like the Law of Attraction, this is a Law of Money. The more money you make, the more you are able to save and the more you are able to give away. The more money you save and the more you give away, the more that money begins to flow back to you. This is the one concept that is usually hard to grasp. How could giving money away help me make more money? I believe that if you are freely giving money from the heart to a charity, your church or any worthy cause, you are in turn sending a message to the universe that you are a generous person and that money is a good and positive thing. I also believe that giving money away freely will provide you with a feeling of gratitude and makes you understand there is a higher cause that needs the money more than you do. When you do this, it feels great and you start to think, "…if I made more money I could really have a big impact from a charitable standpoint…" In turn, you start to discover and the universe starts to deliver, more ways to make money. It is a perpetual cycle that continues to increase in quantity.

<u>Reality</u>

I have posed to you some powerful questions using **The Money Myths**™, **Your Money Relationship**™, **The Money Beliefs**™ and **The Money Flow**™. These will help you understand what money means to you and what money has represented in your life. Given our current economy and uncertain business environment, it is more important than ever before to take responsibility for yourself and stop relying solely on a company, the government, or an institution to ensure your financial stability.

The days of working for a company for 40 years, then retiring with full benefits and a lifetime pension, are coming to an end. The American car manufacturers are a good example. You used to be able to go to work at a car plant out of high school and work there for your whole career. They were going to take care of you no matter what. This is no longer possible or realistic. What about Uncle Sam? Even Social Security could be gone by the time some of us decide to leave the workforce. It is time to get proactive and take control of your financial well-being. It starts with the income you currently earn, how you get paid and how financially responsible you have been to this point. **You need to make the decision right now that you and you alone will take 100% responsibility for your financial security.** The following section on establishing good credit will provide you with some excellent ideas and explain why this is a critical step in establishing financial stability.

The Importance of Good Credit

One of the first things that should be done to get your financial path headed in the right direction is to understand your credit score and how credit works. This is as important for a minimum wage worker as it is for a wealthy business person. Did you know that having a FICO credit score of 720 or higher can actually save you hundreds, even thousands of dollars a month in interest on big items such as your mortgage or your car loans?

Your average FICO score is the one number that can determine what you pay for financing your mortgage, your car and other loans you may need. A good credit score of 720 and higher can allow you to get the best financing for your loan. While a weaker credit score (less than 720) could mean you pay hundreds of dollars more per month for the same financing.

Here are a few things to consider:

- When was the last time you checked your FICO score?
- Do you know what your score is?
- Are there any mistakes in your credit report?
- Over 80% of all credit reports contain errors

I have my own business that generates millions of dollars a year in revenue. This affords me a very comfortable personal income. I pay all of my bills on time and in full and I do not have any credit card debt. I never paid much attention to what my credit score was because I never had to worry about it, or so I thought. But while purchasing a vehicle for my business, I was informed that I would not get the preferred rate because my credit score was only 619. I was astounded and could not figure out how this could be. I thought I had done everything right.

After doing some research online I purchased a program called The 7 Steps to a 720 Credit Score, www.creditscoreto720.com. I followed the program's instructions and confirmed that my FICO score was indeed 619. What immediately caught my attention were the mistakes on the credit report. As I patiently went through the steps outlined in the program, I found out that the credit card companies had combined two of my addresses with incorrect zip codes and because of their mistake my business office had not received statements on several accounts for a period of six months. What this program did was give me a step-by-step process to get these credit card companies to own up to their mistakes and fix my credit reports. Within six weeks my score went from 619 to 740.

Time and Effort versus Results

In today's business world, you can be paid for your time and effort, or for your results, or for a combination of the two. The three examples below outline the different ways you can be paid as an employee:

1) **Employee gets paid for their time and effort**
   Think of an hourly job. You show up, punch a clock and get paid for each hour that you work. If you are making $8 per hour and you work eight hours you make $64 in gross wages for the day.

   High Risk-Low Reward: If you are sick, get hurt off of the job, or have a child-care issue and cannot come to work, you get zero dollars. Most hourly jobs do not include benefits (health, 401(K), vacation, or sick leave).

2) **Employee gets paid a salary**
   Think about a government job. You get a salary of $65,000 per year. You receive a paycheck every two

weeks and you are expected to do a certain amount of work for the money you are being paid.

Low Risk-Moderate Reward-You know what you are going to make every two weeks and this allows you to budget and have some stability. You typically get benefits with this type of arrangement (health, 401(K), vacation, and sick leave)

3) **Employee gets paid a salary + commission/ bonus based on performance**
Think about a stockbroker, insurance broker, sales person, or executive. You typically receive a base salary plus a commission or bonus based on your performance. This gives you the freedom to work as much, as hard, or as smart as you want to and if you produce the expected result or more, your income potential can be unlimited.

Moderate Risk-High Reward-You know what you will make as a base salary every two weeks, and you also have an unlimited upside opportunity to make more based on your output. You typically get benefits with this type of arrangement (health, 401(K), vacation, or sick leave). The other benefit of this type of arrangement, on many occasions, is the freedom to work when and how you want to in order to produce your results. You have some degree of control over how you spend your time.

Where do you stand in the three categories above? Do you currently have an opportunity to control the income you receive based on the results you perform? Do you have control over when and how hard you work? Or do you punch a time clock every day and get paid the same no matter what?

It is important to note that category three does not always have to do with sales. My current company Sharp Details, Inc is a corporate and private aircraft cleaning and support company. Our entire management team gets paid a base salary that allows them to earn a living and then they get a bonus based on the quarterly results of the overall business and their specific location. As the owner, I have an Operations Manager who oversees all day-to-day operations and there are Site Managers at each location. These Site Managers treat their site as if it is their own business: they manage their income, production, supplies, customer service, payroll and staffing. If they produce the desired results, they can increase their annual income by 30-60% through bonuses. As a result of implementing this bonus structure, the business has doubled revenue and profit in the last three years, my job and the job of my Operations Manager have become more efficient and our management team is earning more than they ever did before with our company.

The point is, with a little creativity, being paid for your results instead of your time and effort might well be applicable to your current job or your current business. If you want to increase your income, you must find a way to get yourself into category three (being paid a salary plus a commission or bonus for your results). You will want to think about your current job and see if there is a way you can turn it into one where you can be paid for your results.

Finding a way to increase your current income as quickly as possible is another step to financial stability and financial freedom.

The Financial Stability Table™

The Financial Stability Table™ will assist you in moving to the next step of financial stability and growth. Picture a table with a flat, rectangular top and four sturdy legs. When all four legs of the table are strong, you can sit on it, stack things on it, put your drink on it--you can get many uses from the table. If you take away any of those legs and apply any amount of weight to the table, it will crash to the ground. You still have some premium lumber that can be put to use, but it is no longer a table. Your financial table is the same way. If you are just starting out in your career, think of yourself as a carpenter: you will need to start building your table. If you are well along in your career and you already have a table, always think of ways to reinforce it and make it stronger. Here is what make up the four legs of the table:

Leg 1: Personal Income

This is the income you make every two weeks in the form of a payroll check from your business, the government or the company that employs you.

Leg 2: Savings and other Financial Investments

When investing in these financial vehicles you should take two things into consideration: short term investments in savings and CD accounts and long-term investments such as 401(K) and IRA accounts. Your short term investments will be money that you want to have access to that can be quickly and inexpensively turned into cash. Your long term investments will be investments that you make for retirement or for later in life.

Leg 3: Real Estate Investments

This is equity in the home you live in and/or other properties that you own and any rental income that those properties generate.

Leg 4: Business and Residual Income

This can be income from a business you own or residual income that is continually generated from something you created, as in the case of movie producers, software developers, authors, songwriters and inventors.

The Financial Stability Table™ does several things that will give you the financial stability you deserve:

1) It provides you with multiple streams of income
2) It can provide you with a reserve of immediate cash
3) It gives you diversity in how you invest and how you earn in both short term and long term investment opportunities.
4) It gives you flexibility to move income from one source (securities for example) and invest it into another (real estate or a business opportunity)

Your financial table has four different legs that provide four different income potentials. You must look at each of these in different ways:

Leg #1 is the income you earn every day that enables you to pay your bills, put food on the table, and invest some of that money into Leg #2. Leg #2 is where the money you have earned actually starts to go to work for you. This will give you long term income through compound interest or dividends or securities appreciation. In most cases, Legs #1 and #2 provide a degree of comfort and modest long-term stability if invested correctly. For some people, the stability and comfort this type of income and investing provide may be enough to sustain a very comfortable lifestyle and support you into old age. This may not be enough for those of you that desire complete financial independence and the freedom to do **what you want, when you want, without having to think about the cost.**

Most upper-level individual wealth (net worth of $1 mill +) in America and the world, for that matter, is created through one of two ways: real estate (Leg #3) or owning a business and/or creating residual income (Leg #4). These two avenues have created more millionaires and billionaires than any other wealth creation method that exists. These people are willing to step out on a limb and take the necessary risk in hopes of having very big gains.

Three of the wealthiest people in American history, Bill Gates (Microsoft), Warren Buffet (Berkshire Hathaway), and the late Sam Walton (Wal-Mart), started their own businesses from scratch and created three of the most successful corporations in the world. Bill Gates started what would become Microsoft in his parents' garage after dropping out of college. Warren Buffet bought his first piece of real estate when he was 14 years old. Sam Walton started a five-and-dime store in Arkansas and after five years still only had one small store. You know the rest! These three individuals started out just like you or me and over many years created fortunes beyond imagination. They did not come up with an Internet idea and sell it three years later for $50,000,000 and they did not become financially independent overnight. Although this would be great, it is an extremely rare occurrence. They all started a business with a passion and a dream and that passion and dream led them to create a fortune.

Creating the Mind Set for Wealth

Here are the things I suggest you start doing immediately to get you thinking and acting like someone who is ready to increase their income, improve their financial stability and eventually create lasting wealth and financial independence:

1) Be grateful for what you have and where you are right now (**The Gratitude List**™ from Chapter 3). You must appreciate where you currently are to give yourself the confidence and right frame of mind to move forward.

2) Make the decision that you want to make financial improvements in your life. Set goals for financial stability and control and then set bigger

goals that would describe wealth or financial independence for you.

3) Brainstorm with your spouse, friends, and colleagues and discover new ways to earn additional income.

4) Become more disciplined and learn to live within your means. Cut out frivolous spending on items and services you may not need such as cable channels, new clothes, or memberships. Cut your morning latte and danish ($5 per day during the work week) and you could save $100 per month. Learn to respect and cherish the money you currently earn.

5) Begin training yourself to save 10% of your income every month. It may take time to build up to this level, so start with 2% or 5% and adjust as you can. Even if you are only saving $10 per month it is the consistent discipline of doing this that will become a pattern of behavior as your income increases.

6) Help those less fortunate than you and learn to give away 10% of your income every month. Again, it may take time to build up to this level, so start with 2% or 5% and adjust it as you can. Remember, it the discipline of doing this every month that makes the difference.

7) Surround yourself with people who share the same goals as you, who will support you and who enjoy a lifestyle and income level that you admire and desire.

Today more millionaires are emerging than at any other time in history. People are creating wealth faster and at younger ages every day. There are billionaires in the world that are not yet 30 years old. The Internet and the use of its technology are allowing us to connect to people all over the world in a split second. You can sell an idea or a product or provide consulting to someone who lives in India as easily as someone who lives in Indiana. In the past, your market was in and around your neighborhood; now your market is the world. We are truly living in amazing times.

So what are you going to do with all of this opportunity? What research will you do? What product could you sell? Could you develop a product of your own? My brother created a product from scratch, has a U.S. patent pending and now sells his product to the aviation industry, www.trisoftcovers.com. What could you do, in your spare time to create income, or make extra income? **What are you passionate about**? Could you write a book? Could you create a product in your field of expertise? What are you going to do?

Another step towards improving your current financial situation, creating wealth or striving for financial independence is to define what these things mean to you. It will be different for everyone. What satisfies the needs and goals of a single 45-year-old person will be dramatically different than the goals of a mother and father of four who want all of their kids to attend college. No matter what your career or where you are financially, you need to answer the following questions to gain clarity on where you are and where you want to go financially. The answers to these questions will vary for everyone. My goal here is to shift your thinking from a point of financial stability to a place of financial independence:

- What amount of money would you need to earn each year to feel **financially stable**? At this level, you may not be able to have the vacation or car you want, but all of your basic needs would be met and all bills would be paid.
- What amount of money would you need to earn each year to feel **financially satisfied**? At this level you can afford the home you want, all of your basic needs and bills are paid. You are investing for college (if necessary); you are saving 10% and giving away 10% of your income.
- What amount of money would you have to earn each year to feel **financially independent**? At this level, you can afford the home, vacation and car you want, all basic needs and bills are paid. You are investing for college (if necessary); you are saving 10% and giving away 10% of your income. You are also able to afford other luxuries like a second home, additional vacations, additional giving to charities or your church and you can do pretty much what you want without thinking too much about the financial impact it may have.
- Does or will your current job or business give you the income potential you need or the opportunity in the future to earn the income you de-

sire and reach any or all of the levels described above?

- What else could you do to earn additional income at your current job, with your current business, or by starting something new?

- Try to imagine how good it would feel if all of your bills were paid each month, your retirement plans were funded, you donated to the charities of your choice and you still had an extra $2000, $5000, or $10,000 per month left over. What could you do with the extra money?

- Finally, for those of you who have huge financial dreams and aspirations, what amount of money would you need to earn to feel truly **financially free**? At this level, you could do whatever you wanted, whenever you wanted without ever having to consider the financial impact on your life.

- No matter what your level of earning right now, imagine and write down how it would feel if you did not have to worry about money, ever again.

Your answers to these questions should help you begin to understand what actions you need to take in order to change your financial situation. Even with a successful business, I have started to develop joint ventures, writing opportunities, online businesses, affiliate associations, consulting, speaking engagements and real estate investing as various additional streams of income for my family and me. All of these opportunities are based on the experiences I have had and the lessons

I have learned while growing my own small business. The more sources of income you can create and control, the more stable your financial future becomes and the greater your chances to achieve real wealth.

Start Your Own Business

Starting your own business is easier than most people would imagine. It can all be done online, so you can avoid having to go to your local and state judicial buildings. There are many tax advantages to having your own business that make it worth the cost (which is generally only a few hundred dollars.) The beauty of starting your own part-time business is that you can continue working your current job and have the income, stability and benefits that job provides. When I started Barnacle Jim's Boat Service, the company that is now known as Sharp Details, Inc. back in 1991 I had no money. I worked on my business during the day and waited tables five-seven nights a week.

Here are a few things to consider when starting your own business:

- Do you have a passion? What are your hobbies and interests? What experiences have you had or obstacles have you overcome? Are you an expert at anything?
- Can you start the business in your spare time?
- Can you keep your current job and source of income?

- Perform online research through Google, Ask and other search engines to see if there is a demand for your idea or area of expertise
- Set up the business as an LLC (Limited Liability Corporation)--this will keep you and your business as two separate entities
- Start a low-cost business (consulting, re-selling, writing, or marketing) so you get paid for what you know, not what you can do

There are amazing resources available today that can assist you in starting your own business. With a computer and the Internet you can instantly find what businesses and services are needed today, how to start a business, how to write a business plan, how to market your business, how to make a web page and how to sell on line--the information is endless. Check out the resources page on our web site www.theprac-ticalguidetoexceptionalliving.com it will provide you with tools to start and set up your own business and will assist you in taking that first, big step.

I understand that some people are not interested in having their own business because of the high risk and exposure they may be faced with or they do not want to manage employees, or perhaps they do not feel like they have the time. But here is something to think about: What are your hobbies?

- Do you enjoy photography? Start a photography business. Now you can write off the cost of your film, fancy camera, and some vehicle mileage, and earn extra income working parties, weddings, doing custom photography for friends or selling stock photos online.

- Do you like to run? Start a running club with membership dues that are paid monthly. Start an online business that re-sells running supplies like shoes, socks, running clothes, and maps of different running routes in different cities.

- Are you an attorney? Perhaps you are tired of the big law firm, the demanding partners, and long hours. Start a consulting business where you get paid to give legal advice at rates and hours that you set. Maybe you decide to work four days per week and take Fridays off. If it is your business, you can do what you want.

These are just a few examples of how you could develop a business out of a hobby or area of expertise. It does not have to be a fortune-building enterprise like Microsoft or Wal-Mart. Your new business could simply be something that allows you to earn an extra $2000-$3000 per month and enjoy your passion while getting paid. You can do all of this while continuing to work your full time job and enjoy the stability, income and benefits that it brings. Remember, it is up to you to decide exactly what it is you want financially.

Chapter Five Summary
The Money Dance

Key Points to Remember

- Eliminate the Money Myths™ from your thinking

- Understand your current Money Relationship™, how it has impacted your life to this point and what you need to do to improve it

- Understand your Money Beliefs™ and how those beliefs have impacted you financially, eliminate any negative beliefs you have about money and wealth

- Begin following The Money Flow™ rules today

- Give away 10% of your income to charities, your church and those less fortunate

- Discover a way to get paid for your results (commission and bonuses) and not for your time and effort (salary and hourly)

- Take the necessary steps to raise your FICO credit score to 720 or higher
  www.creditscoreto720.com

- Study the Financial Money Table™ and develop a strategy to begin growing each leg of the table

- Develop a strategy to develop multiple streams of income and residual income through writing, starting a business or developing a product

- Start your own home-based business around a hobby, a passion, your professional experience, consulting or a need in society

- Determine the exact amount of additional income you would need to become financially secure and envision yourself in a position where you do not have to worry about money each month

- Take ACTION and do one thing today that would start you on your path to financial independence

Please answer the following questions. Challenging yourself to answer the "why"_after each question will give you the justification to continue that behavior...or make the effort to change.

- What is your current relationship with and belief about money? Why?

- Was money ever an issue or problem in your family? Why?

- Did you always have plenty of money growing up or was it a challenge? Why?

- Did your parents come from money, were they self-made or did they struggle? Why?

- Do you have enough money to do all of the things you want to do in your life? Why or why not?

- Do you make money while you sleep or do you have to work for it? Why?

- Are you saving enough money for your future, kids' education and retirement? Why or why not?

- Do you save 10% and give away 10% of your income each month? Why or why not?

- Do you get paid for your time and effort (hourly or salary) or do you get paid for the results you produce (bonus or commission)? Why or why not?

- Do you know your FICO score and do you have a current credit report? Why?

- How many streams of income do you currently have? Why?

- Do you have a passion, hobby or field of expertise that could lead you to start your own business?

- What additional amount of money would you need each month to cover all expenses and investment commitments and still have $3,000-$5,000 leftover to do with what you wish?

- What would you do with an additional $3,000-$5,000 extra each month? Why?

- If you became wealthy, earning $300,000-$500,000+ per year, what positive impact could you have on your community, society and the world?

Chapter Six
The Life of Your Dreams:
Setting and Reaching Your Goals

"Give me a stock clerk with a goal and I'll give you a man who will make history. Give me a man with no goals and I'll give you a stock clerk."
James Cash Penny (1875-1971)
Founder, JC Penny Company

 This chapter will teach you how to set your goals and develop a plan to make those goals a reality.

The Two Things That Can Stop You from Reaching Your Goals

What you must realize today is that you have to change your perception of reality and what got you to this point in your life. You must accept the fact that only two things have kept you from really breaking out and going after BIG goals and dreams which cause you to stretch and expand your horizons. These two things are:

Your Thoughts and Fear

I have talked about your thoughts and what impact they have on you in every chapter of this book. How you think and what you expect is what you will become and what you will get in life. Your thoughts control how you act every day. If you are *afraid* of failure, this *fear* will stop you in your tracks.

If you think about *scarcity and lack* and *what you don't have,* you will take actions that are *conservative and restrictive* because *you don't have enough* and you can't bear to think about losing what *little* you have. Your thinking will be *small* and your circle of influence will be *critical of your dreams and restrictive* in thought and advice. Does this sound fun and exciting? Absolutely not!

If you think about *abundance and are grateful*, you will take actions that are *bold and exciting* because *you will appreciate what you have* and you will be *excited* and *fearless* about creating an *abundant future*. Your thinking will be BIG and your circle of influence will be *supportive and motivating*. Does this sound fun and exciting? YES!!

The Two Questions That Will Allow You to Accomplish Anything

You must learn to ask yourself the right questions in every aspect of your life if you are going to accomplish what you truly want. You must also become a master of your feelings and your emotions. Mastering these two things will give you the power to overcome your negative thoughts and your fears. Here are the two most important questions you have to ask yourself:

Why?

It is the *why* that will give you the emotional state to go ahead with big plans and accomplish your dreams.

Imagine a life of great health and longevity, a positive attitude, turning failure into opportunity, the ability to do whatever you want whenever you want, financial freedom, the ability to travel and experience different cultures and most of all the time to spend with the people you love. Is this what you would truly like to have? *Why?*

How would that make you feel?

It is the *feelings* you will get from creating an abundant life that make it all worth the effort. It is the *feelings* that will be created once you have accomplished your biggest goals that will have the greatest impact on your life. For clarity I will use great health and longevity as an example:

Why would you want great health and longevity? So you can have the energy to spend time with the people you love. So you can live to be 100 and spend time with the grandkids and great-grand kids. So you can have more time to do all of the things you want to do. So you can experience more things in life. So you can have a greater impact on society. So you can do all of the physical activities you want without being exhausted.

How would it feel to have great health and longevity? It would *feel* great. It would give you peace of mind knowing you were reducing your health risks. It would be a good example to set for others. It would give you the security to know you would be here to take care of your family. It would be exciting to have the energy to do what you want. It would be powerful to have control over your body and mind. And most of all, it would be the self confidence you would gain from mastering the discipline needed to accomplish your goals!

Having a full understanding of this concept is crucial in giving you the emotional power and confidence to create and live the life of your dreams. You must be clear about the reasons why a goal is important to you and have enough emotion tied to the realization of that goal. Then nothing will stop you. You will accomplish it, no matter what.

Setting Goals

Setting goals is a process that requires attention to detail and creativity. You must be willing to eliminate obstacles and roadblocks and let your mind run free. This is the time to dream and think BIG. It does not matter how crazy a goal may seem or how impossible it may seem at this point in your life. You must find that childlike imagination that still resides in all of us and let it run wild. And once this is done, you must *TAKE IMMEDIATE AND MASSIVE ACTION!*

Setting goals is a four step process:

1) The Mind Dump™

The purpose of **The Mind Dump™** is to get as many ideas and goals as you can onto a sheet of paper in five minutes. You let your mind flow and forget about any and all limitations.

- To do this exercise you will need a legal pad, pen, and a timer or stopwatch
- I want you to take a few minutes and think of everything you ever wanted to be, do or have

- This should include ideas you have for relationships, finances, travel, health, spirituality, houses, cars, time, and your career
- Don't consider any restrictions you currently have - just dream and think BIG!
- Set the timer for five minutes and write everything down that pops into your head as quickly as you can. Do not worry about order, just write it down.
- When you have completed this exercise, you should have a long list of all the things you ever wanted to be, do, or have. If ideas are still coming to you after five minutes, continue writing.

2) The Goal Filter™

The Goal Filter™ is a form to help you organize all of your thoughts and goals. It can be downloaded from my website www.thepracticalguidetoexceptionalliving. com. This form will allow you to group all of your goals into categories that include relationships, career, health, finances, wealth, time, travel and adventure and other items you may want (cars, houses, clothes, and toys).

- Take all of your ideas from **The Mind Dump**™ and put them in the proper category on your worksheet.
- When you have all of your goals categorized, assign a number in order of importance to each item you wrote down (#1 being the most important goal in each category).
- Starting with your favorite category, write down your #1 goal from each category on a separate

sheet of paper. When you do this, be very deliberate in making sure that your handwriting is very neat and legible.

• This is the starting point for all of your goals moving forward. I asked you to write down your health goals first because this is the most important goal to fulfill to get mentally and physically prepared to work towards your other goals.

3) The Goal Card™

The Goal Card™ helps you break down each goal and get specific about what it is that you want to accomplish. It also helps create a timeframe for completing each goal and what action is necessary to achieve your goal. The other key to this exercise is to write everything down as if it has already been accomplished. You want to trick the mind into thinking you have already achieved this goal. Remember the Law of Attraction from Chapter 4? It states that you will achieve what you believe.

To make a **Goal Card™** do the following:

1) Get a clean sheet of paper
2) Write down your exact goal and the planned (desired) date of accomplishment
3) Write down what you have had to do or give to accomplish your goal
4) Write down why this goal is important to you
5) Write down the plan you had to follow to accomplish this goal
6) Write down how accomplishing this goal has changed your life

7) Write down what emotions you felt when you accomplished this goal

8) Combine all of this information and condense it onto a 3X5 card

9) Look at this card every night and every morning. While looking at the card, close your eyes and imagine your goal as already accomplished. Carry the card with you and look at it during the day or keep it taped to your bathroom mirror or on your dashboard.

Use this acronym to make sure you have incorporated all of the key points into your goal-setting exercise.

SMART: Specific – Measurable – Attainable – Relevant – Timely

Below is an example:

It is October 10, and your goal is to lose 25 pounds. This is great but you need to be more specific. You might say, " I want to lose 25 pounds in the next six months (specific) by March 10, (timely & attainable) because I want to be back in a size six, have more energy and feel great (relevant). Following this plan I have to lose 1 pound per week (measurable & attainable). This way I can wear my old clothes, buy some new ones and have more fun with the kids at the pool this summer." This last sentence is where the emotion of achieving the goal comes into play. At this point you have a concrete goal with all of the components in place. Now you have to describe you and your situation as if it has already been accomplished.

This is how your **Goal Card**™ may look for the above example. Remember to write the goal as if it has already been accomplished:

> **It is March 10, (YEAR) and I have lost 25 pounds**
>
> I am so proud of myself for sticking to my exercise program and eating plan. I have continued to work out and move forward with my plan. It is March 10, (Year) and I have lost the 25 lbs. I feel great. I am wearing clothes that I have not worn in years. My husband says I look great and my friends can't believe the results I have had. I feel confident and strong and I am proud of myself for having the courage and the discipline to accomplish this goal. I can't wait to get to the pool and the beach this summer.

4) Manage Your Expectations

Don't forget to be patient with yourself and allow the time needed to achieve your goals.

My good friend and CFO, Tom Dula, is always reminding me to manage my expectations. He encourages me to be patient with myself and not to get discouraged if my plans do not take off as quickly as I would like. Everyone thinks differently and has different expectations. Some realize it may take a year or two to realize a goal; others (I fall into this category) expect to see results immediately. I can tell you from experience that big goals take time and little goals usually do not. If you set a big goal, as in the example above, you must break it down to the smaller things you can do each day. This way you have something to celebrate every day. This will keep you excited and confident to reach the big goal.

Think about the process of a baby learning how to walk:

1) The baby learns to raise up on its hands
2) Then the baby learns to roll over
3) Then it learns to roll back
4) Then it finally gets to its hands and knees
5) For a long time the baby rocks back and forth
6) Then one day the baby crawls a few feet
7) The baby continues to practice until it can crawl well
8) Then the baby pulls itself up
9) The baby falls a lot and cries and gets discouraged, but never quits trying to pull itself up
10) Then one day, the baby takes a step…then two… and then three and before you know it, the baby is walking
11) A baby's entire existence is transformed once it can get around and begin exploring its new world

A baby has just achieved its first big goal as a human and it does not even know that it has been through a process to accomplish this. It is done by instinct and not on a conscious level. If any of you have witnessed this with your own kids, it is a remarkable experience. As parents, we help them, we cheer for them, we help catch them when they stumble, we tell our friends and we take a video. This is a big deal!

For the baby the goal was to walk. It took many steps and setbacks and much pain and frustration to get there, but the baby does not know it can quit. The baby always keeps trying. As adults we need to do the same. You will surely be met with obstacles on your journey towards your big goals. When you stumble and fall you must be able to get up, dust yourself off and continue moving forward.

What I want you to remember is you must do something every day to get you a little closer to your goal. For me, writing this book started with an idea and it took me 10 years to finally obtain the discipline and the time to sit down and write it. It was a long, sometimes frustrating and painful process, but ultimately it has been very satisfying. This book was written, edited, re-written and re-edited many times. It has been a process like anything else and processes take time.

Flexibility

Setting goals (of any size) requires flexibility. You are inevitably going to start out towards your goal in one direction and try to get from point A to point B rather quickly and directly. This rarely happens. I can say without pause that every goal I have set out to achieve has involved many detours, digressions and deviations before it is realized. Many factors affect our path: employees come and go, customers change, financial situations fluctuate, family events occur, babies are born, holidays come up and new opportunities present themselves. You must remain flexible and understand that the path to your goal will be fluid and that is OK. Just do not lose focus on the ultimate goal. Always know where you are headed. **Set the goal, check your** results at timely intervals along the way and change your plan if you are not getting the results you want.

The Law of Attraction

We discussed the Law of Attraction in Chapter 4. Some people are not comfortable with this Law--it is a little too kooky for them. **I beg you to consider what I am telling you here.** You will attract into your life whatever it is you are most predominantly thinking about every day. I am not a metaphysical nut job; I am a successful, educated and seasoned entrepreneur who has created the life of my dreams. The Law of Attraction is the single biggest factor that I can attribute to my success. When I finally grasped this, understood it completely and trusted in it, my whole life changed. You must continually focus and think about what you want and keep your mind away from the obstacles, challenges and roadblocks that you will encounter. When you begin your goal writing process, you must immediately begin thinking about having this goal accomplished and how you will feel once you have completed your journey. This will attract the right resources and the right people at the right time to help move you towards your goal. In particular, key people will start to show up in your life. For example, a trainer might appear if you are trying to lose weight, or a friend calls and says there is a new job opening at their company. Whatever it is, if you hold that goal out there and think about it as already having been achieved, then you will start to draw to you the people and resources you need to achieve it. You have to trust me on this!

The Circle of Attraction™

The **Circle of Attraction**™ is another factor you must begin to consider if you are going to achieve big things in your life. Who do you hang out with? Who are the people you spend much of your time with? Who do you talk with at work? Who do you associate with in your neighborhood? Are these people helping you reach your goals? Are they rooting for you? Are they being positive and supportive? Have any of them reached some of the goals that you want to achieve? This is your desired **Circle of Attraction**™. These are the people you associate with every day.

Maybe your goal is to make $200,000 a year, but you have never made more than $75,000. Everybody you hang out with makes $75,000 or less and you do not know anyone who makes $200,000 a year. You have to start looking for mentors, people who have achieved your desired goal and would be willing to help you. Who in your community, at your church or at your child's school makes that kind of money? What do they do for a living? What do they read? Where do they go out to eat? If you observe the activities of those who earn at this level and you start modeling some of their behaviors, you will start getting some of the same results.

This is extremely important for health as well. If you are overweight and want to get in better shape, you need to find someone who used to be heavy and who is now fit and you need to model their behavior. Do the same types of things that they do. That's **The Circle of Attraction**™.

What If I Succeed?

As we discussed earlier in this chapter, fear can be an emotion that holds you back. Both fear of failure and, as described here, fear of success or fear of being judged for your success. What if you are able to set huge goals and achieve them? For me, early on, that was a scary prospect. That is where **fear of being judged by others comes** into play. *"Gosh, what if I did achieve these things? How would people judge me? What would people think about me? What if I earn more money than my father ever did? What if I earn more money than anyone else in my family ever did?"* I used to struggle with these fears and had a problem with how I would be judged if I succeeded.

What I have learned is that success for one breeds success for others. And it is OK to make a lot of money. Just remember the more you make, the more you give and contribute.

The greatest gift you can give society is to strive for success. The more you achieve on every level and the happier you are with your life, the more positively you will influence those around you---your family, friends, colleagues and society as a whole.

Follow your dreams and encourage others to do the same. You, your family, your community and the world will be better for it.

Chapter Six Summary
The Life of Your Dreams:
Setting and Reaching Your Goals

Key Points to Remember

- Thoughts of negativity, doubt and fear can keep you from reaching your goals

- Constantly ask the questions "Why?" and "How does this make me feel?" The answers to these will guide you toward your goal

- Setting goals is like any other process and must incorporate your imagination

- The Mind Dump™ requires five minutes to write down all of your goals and dreams

- The Goal Filter™ will help you organize and categorize your goals

- The Goal Card™ is your index card for each goal with all of the details and plans condensed

- Goals must be S.M.A.R.T. Specific – Measurable – Attainable – Relevant - Timely

- Manage your expectations and be patient with yourself

- Break your goal down into smaller action items you can do each day or each week

- Think about the baby learning to walk and how little actions over time can accomplish a big goal

- Be flexible on the path to your goal and understand that your original plan may change along the way

- Utilize The Law of Attraction and The Circle of Attraction™ to obtain the knowledge, skills and information needed to achieve your goals

- Understand that your success is the greatest gift you can give to others and to yourself

Please answer the following questions. Challenging yourself to answer the "why" after each question will give you the justification to continue that behavior...or choose to change.

- What goals do you have that you have never pursued? Why or why not?

- Do you believe you can accomplish big goals? Why or why not?

- Are you afraid of trying to go after a BIG goal? Why?

- Are you afraid of how you might be judged by others if you succeed? Why?

- What are your three biggest goals right now in your life? Why?

- How would it make you feel if you were able to accomplish your three biggest goals? Why?

- What could you contribute to society if you accomplished your biggest goals? Why?

- Have you ever actually written goals down? Why or why not?

- How would you describe your current Circle of Attraction™?

- Is your current Circle of Attraction™ going to allow you to reach your goals? Why or why not?

- Do you know anyone who has done or accomplished the things you want to do and accomplish?

- What action could you take today to get you going in the direction of your goals?

- Do you feel confident that you can accomplish your goals? Why or why not?

- What other resources, tools and information will you need to accomplish your goals? Why?

Chapter Seven
Proof and Resources

"That some achieve great success is proof to all that others can achieve it as well."
Abraham Lincoln (1809-1865)
16th President of the United States

In closing, I would like to leave you with three stories where humble beginnings were turned into great successes by those who were considered "too young," "too old," or "not educated enough" to achieve their dreams, but did so anyway. I have also listed suggested readings on a variety of the subjects covered in this book.

Sam Walton (1918-1992) American Businessman

Sam Walton may be regarded as one of the greatest businessmen to ever live. He started with one five-and-dime store in 1945. When his lease was not renewed in 1950, he was forced to sell his inventory and fixtures to the landlord. He then opened his first "Walton's 5 and 10" operated under a franchise agreement with Chicago's Ben Franklin. By 1962, Sam and his brother had grown the operation to 16 stores throughout Arkansas, Missouri and Oklahoma.

The first Wal-Mart opened in 1962, when Sam was 44 years old. Sam outmatched the competition and set himself apart by offering low prices, variety, clean stores, friendly staff and extended hours. By the end of the century, Wal-Mart was the world's largest retailer. The company now operates 7400 facilities worldwide. What started as a small five-and-dime in the middle of America has become a company that employs 2,000,000 people and generated $347 billion in revenue in 2008.

Some may think of Wal-Mart as big and greedy; however, Wal-Mart generously gives back every year to local community programs and international outreach companies. **In 2007 the Wal-Mart stores, Sam's Clubs and the Wal-Mart Foundation gave more than $296 million to 4000+ communities in the U.S. and had international donations that topped $41 million.**

Sam Walton was an ordinary man like you or me. He was not exceptionally gifted nor did he come from a lot of money. Through his vision, ingenuity, ability to hire the right people and use of technology, Sam Walton was able to create the largest retail operation in the world and at the same time create one of the biggest contributors and givers to the world as well. www.walmart.com

Justin Sachs (1989 -) Personal Development Coach, Entrepreneur, and Author

Justin Sachs started in the personal development industry at the age of 13 by attending his first Anthony Robbins seminar. It was then that he realized he wanted to help others. He started a non-profit organization, Peak

Performance Lifestyles Foundation, at the age of 16 to help teenagers develop their leadership skills through developing community service teams in their neighborhoods. Encouraged by the success of his Foundation, Justin started Motivational Press, Inc., a publishing and media company and published his first book, *Your Mailbox Is Full- Real Teens in the Real World*. This guidebook gives teenagers every tool, strategy and principle they need for success in school and throughout life. Justin also developed the "Motivational Minds Radio show," bringing the greatest leaders in personal and business development to his listeners in a weekly online radio show. Justin most recently founded Peak Performance Lifestyles Inc., his leadership coaching and international speaking company. Justin travels the world coaching and training teenagers and young adults to become leaders that create change in their communities.

Justin is just 20 years old!!

Email: justinsachs@mac.com
Website: www.JSachs.com

Harland "Colonel" Sanders (1890-1980) Restaurateur and Franchiser

Harland Sanders grew up in a poor family in Indiana during the early 1900's. He worked his first job at the age of ten at a nearby farm and by sixth grade had quit school to help support his family.

From ages 16-40, Sanders worked as an insurance salesman, operated a river boat company, served as a secretary for the Columbus Chamber of Commerce, launched a manufacturing company (which failed), earned his law degree and started a law practice (which also eventually failed). In 1929, he started a small restaurant that did well and later opened a hotel, service station and second restaurant across the street. Sanders, was given the honorary title of "Kentucky Colonel" by the governor of Kentucky, Ruby Laffoon in 1935. He took an eight week course in restaurant and hotel management to learn more about the business. In 1937, he tried to open a chain of restaurants, but failed. In 1939, he opened another restaurant and motel and it, too, failed.

But Sanders was determined and in 1939 he also perfected a method for cooking his fried chicken with his secret recipe. By the 1950's he had signed up a few restaurants as franchisees to sell his chicken. He was paid five cents for every chicken cooked with his recipe.

In 1956, at the age of 66, Sanders was almost broke and living off of his Social Security check. He packed up his car and started traveling all over the south to find franchisees that would cook and sell his chicken. Four years later, Sanders had 400 franchisees and was making $300,000 per year, and by 1964 he sold the enterprise to investors for $2,000,000. In 1986 "Kentucky Fried Chicken" (KFC) was sold to Pepsi for $840 million.

I use these examples to show you that you are never too young or too old to start a business and go after your dreams. These three people came from meager beginnings without a lot of role models and found a way to make a difference in their own lives, the lives of their families and the lives of so many others. An owner of a five-and-dime store, a 20 year old kid with a high school education, and a 66 year old with a sixth grade education--they achieved great things in their lives because they never quit, did not let their age stop them, never stopped trying and kept their eye on their goals.

This book was designed and written to get you thinking about your life and your future and the possibilities that exist for you and for others in the world today. My hope is that I have succeeded in my mission.

In closing I will leave you with two very important questions:

If you knew that you could not fail, what would you try to accomplish?

What are YOU going to do now?

www.thepracticalguidetoexceptionalliving.com

THE
PRACTICAL GUIDE
TO EXCEPTIONAL LIVING
CREATING AND LIVING THE LIFE OF YOUR DREAMS

Special Offer!

Thank you for reading "The Practical Guide to Exceptional Living", I hope you have enjoyed the ideas and concepts that were shared and that you have learned something exceptional that you can put to use right now. Here is a special offer that I have created just for you.

You will receive the following:

- The audio version of The Practical Guide to Exceptional Living

- A copy of The Practical Guide to Exceptional Living workbook.

- An introduction (2 days) to my new 14 day online training program called The Predictable Future™.

- Other bonus material that you can begin using today.

Please go to
www.thepracticalguidetoexceptionalliving.com/specialoffer

You will receive this special offer, a $139 value absolutely free.

The Practical Guide to Exceptional Living
Resource Guide

Suggested Reading

Faith and The Law of Attraction

- *Think and Grow Rich* – Napoleon Hill
- *The Secret* – Rhonda Byrne
- *The Purpose Driven Life* – Rick Warren
- *The Power of Positive Thinking* – Norman Vincent Peale

Health

- *Green for Life* – Victoria Boutenko
- *The Heart Revolution* – Kilmer McCully, MD
- *The Blue Zones* – Dan Buettner
- *Force of Nature* – Laird Hamilton
- *Body for Life* – Bill Phillips

Business

- *The E-Myth* – Michael Gerber
- *The Strategic Coach Program* – www.strategiccoach.com
- *Straight from the Gut* – Jack Welch
- *Good to Great* – Jim Collins
- *The 4-Hour Work Week* – Timothy Ferris

<u>**Finances and Money**</u>

- *The Richest Man in Babylon* – George Clason
- *The Automatic Millionaire* – David Bach
- *The Wealthy Barber* – David Chilton

You can also find many helpful resources and tools at the web pages listed below that I have created to help you along your journey.

- For tools on creating your extraordinary life: www.thepracticalguidetoexceptionalliving.com
- Check out my blog: www.jim-garland.com
- For business consulting, key-note speaking and webinar information: www.garlandcommunication.com
- To learn more about Sharp Details, Inc.: www.sharpdetails.com

BUY A SHARE OF THE FUTURE IN YOUR COMMUNITY

These certificates make great holiday, graduation and birthday gifts that can be personalized with the recipient's name. The cost of one S.H.A.R.E. or one square foot is $54.17. The personalized certificate is suitable for framing and will state the number of shares purchased and the amount of each share, as well as the recipient's name. The home that you participate in "building" will last for many years and will continue to grow in value.

HABITAT FOR HUMANITY

THIS CERTIFIES THAT

<u>YOUR NAME HERE</u>

HAS INVESTED IN A HOME FOR A DESERVING FAMILY

1985-2005

TWENTY YEARS OF BUILDING FUTURES IN OUR
COMMUNITY ONE HOME AT A TIME

1200 SQUARE FOOT HOUSE @ $65,000 = $54.17 PER SQUARE FOOT
This certificate represents a tax deductible donation. It has no cash value.

Here is a sample SHARE certificate:

YES, I WOULD LIKE TO HELP!

I support the work that Habitat for Humanity does and I want to be part of the excitement! As a donor, I will receive periodic updates on your construction activities but, more importantly, I know my gift will help a family in our community realize the dream of homeownership. **I would like to SHARE in your efforts against substandard housing in my community!** *(Please print below)*

PLEASE SEND ME _____ SHARES at $54.17 EACH = $ $_____

In Honor Of: _____

Occasion: (Circle One)   *HOLIDAY*   *BIRTHDAY*   *ANNIVERSARY*

     OTHER: _____

Address of Recipient: _____

Gift From: _____ *Donor Address:* _____

Donor Email: _____

I AM ENCLOSING A CHECK FOR $ $_____ PAYABLE TO HABITAT FOR HUMANITY OR PLEASE CHARGE MY VISA OR MASTERCARD *(CIRCLE ONE)*

Card Number _____ Expiration Date: _____

Name as it appears on Credit Card _____ Charge Amount $ _____

Signature _____

Billing Address _____

Telephone # Day _____ Eve _____

PLEASE NOTE: Your contribution is tax-deductible to the fullest extent allowed by law.
Habitat for Humanity • P.O. Box 1443 • Newport News, VA 23601 • 757-596-5553
www.HelpHabitatforHumanity.org

Printed in the USA
CPSIA information can be obtained
at www.ICGtesting.com
JSHW082212140824
68134JS00014B/583